Patriot Act

LANDMARK LEGISLATION
Patriot Act

Rebecca Stefoff

mc **Marshall Cavendish**
Benchmark
New York

With thanks to Catherine McGlone, Esq., for her expert review of this manuscript.

Other Marshall Cavendish Offices:
Marshall Cavendish International (Asia) Private Limited, 1 New Industrial Road, Singapore
536196 • Marshall Cavendish International (Thailand) Co. Ltd., 253 Asoke, 12th Flr,
Sukhumvit 21 Road, Klongtoey Nua, Wattana, Bangkok 10110, Thailand • Marshall
Cavendish (Malaysia) Sdn Bhd, Times Subang, Lot 46, Subang Hi-Tech Industrial Park, Batu
Tiga, 40000 Shah Alam, Selangor Darul Ehsan, Malaysia

Marshall Cavendish is a trademark of Times Publishing Limited

All websites were available and accurate when this book was sent to press.
"From Bill to Law" is used by permission of Susan Dudley Gold.

Library of Congress Cataloging-in-Publication Data
Stefoff, Rebecca.
The Patriot Act / by Rebecca Stefoff.
p. cm. — (Landmark legislation)
Includes bibliographical references and index.
ISBN 978-1-60870-042-4 (alk. paper)
1. United States. Uniting and Strengthening America by Providing Appropriate Tools
Required to Intercept and Obstruct Terrorism (USA PATRIOT ACT) Act of 2001—Juvenile
literature. 2. Terrorism—United States—Prevention—Juvenile literature. 3. War on
Terrorism, 2001—Law and legislation—United States—Juvenile literature. I. Title.
KF9430.S74 2011
345.73'02—dc22

2009032232

Publisher: Michelle Bisson
Art Director: Anahid Hamparian
Series Designer: Sonia Chaghatzbanian
Photo research by Candlepants, Inc.

Cover photo: President George W. Bush signs the Patriot Act into law on October 26, 2001,
six weeks after the 9/11 terrorist attack on two American cities.

The photographs in this book are used by permission and through the courtesy of: Shawn
Thew/AFP/Getty Images, cover, 2; Christophe Simon/AFP, 3, 112; Eric Draper/White
House, 6; Stephen Jaffe/AFP, 14; Joyce Naltchayan/AFP, 23; Scott J. Ferrell/Congressional
Quarterly, 24; Hulton Archive, 36, 59; Time Life Pictures/Mansell/Time Life Pictures, 61;
Robert Nickelsberg, 70; Roberto Schmidt/AFP, 97; Saul Loeb/AFP, 126; Illini Studio: 67;
Corbis: Michael Maloney/San Francisco Chronicle, 84.

Printed in Malaysia (T)
1 3 5 6 4 2

Contents

President George W. Bush was reading to schoolchildren in a Sarasota, Florida, classroom when he got the news about the attack on the World Trade Center. Here, he makes a phone call to discuss the situation while director of communications Dan Bartlett points to a television set replaying the damage to the Twin Towers.

CHAPTER ONE

Fiery Beginnings

In early 2001 an attorney named Viet Dinh went to work at the Department of Justice in Washington, D.C., where he held the post of assistant attorney general. Well versed in constitutional law, Dinh was responsible for helping to shape federal legal policy in such areas as drug trafficking, racial profiling, and child abuse. He worked under John Ashcroft, the attorney general of the United States and the head of the Justice Department. Like Ashcroft, Dinh was committed to helping the crime-fighting efforts of law enforcement and intelligence agencies such as the Federal Bureau of Investigation and the Central Intelligence Agency.

By September 11, 2001, Dinh had been at his new job for just a few months. That morning he ate breakfast, as usual, at a Washington restaurant favored by people from the Justice Department, the White House, and other branches of the government. At 9:30 a.m., Dinh was on his fourth cup of coffee, having a lively conversation with colleagues. A young man ran up to the table and blurted, "A plane has crashed. It hit the World Trade Center." An instant later, a chorus of beeps broke out around the table—everyone's pager or cell phone had sounded at once. The situation was clearly a crisis.

Dinh hurried to his office. When he got there, he found that the Justice Department, like most government buildings in Washington, was being evacuated. The World Trade Center in New York City was not the only place that had been struck by a plane that morning. The Pentagon had been hit, and authorities feared that other Washington landmarks would follow. U.S. Air Force fighter jets roared through the sky above the capital, patrolling the area.

Government employees were urged to return home, so Dinh went to his house in Chevy Chase, Maryland, outside the capital. Within a few hours several colleagues from the Justice Department had joined him there. They sat in a sun-washed room and stared in shock and anger at the images on Dinh's television. The United States had just suffered one of the few terrorist attacks in its history—and the worst.

Earlier that day nineteen terrorists had seized control of four airplanes and made a coordinated attack on New York and Washington landmarks. They flew three of the planes into buildings: the two towers of the World Trade Center in New York, and the Pentagon, the headquarters of the U.S. military, in Washington. The fourth hijacked airplane plunged to the ground near the town of Shanksville, Pennsylvania. Evidence from cell phone calls made before the crash suggests that some of the passengers on the plane had struggled with the hijackers, who then lost control of the aircraft. No one knows their intended target, but it may have been another Washington landmark, perhaps the Capitol building or the White House.

ATTACK ON AMERICA

On the day that has come to be known as 9/11, President George W. Bush awoke in Florida, where he was scheduled to spend part of the morning reading to a classroom of second-graders in Sarasota. As Bush's motorcade arrived at the school, his advisers received word that minutes earlier, at 8:46 a.m., an airplane had flown into the North Tower, one of two skyscrapers at the World Trade Center in New York City. The president assumed that the crash was an accident, telling Andrew Card, his chief of staff, "The guy [pilot] must have had a heart attack."

At 9:05 a.m. President Bush was sitting on a stool in the classroom, talking with the students, when Card leaned close to the president and whispered the latest news from New York: "A second plane hit the second tower. America is under attack." As soon as Bush heard this shocking news, he formed a firm resolve. "They had declared war on us," he said later, "and I made up my mind at that moment that we were going to war."

But who were "they"? Who had attacked the United States? By midafternoon the president had been flown to a secure underground bunker in Nebraska. From there he held a conference call with key figures in his administration. The terrorists' background was supplied by George Tenet, director of the Central Intelligence Agency, which is the arm of government charged with gathering intelligence, or information, about foreign governments and operatives. "Sir," Tenet told the president, "I believe it's al-Qaeda. . . . [I]t looks like, it feels like, it smells like al-Qaeda."

Tenet was referring to an international network of Islamic extremists headed by Osama bin Laden, who, born in Saudi Arabia, had had his Saudi citizenship revoked in 1994 because of threats to overturn the government. Al-Qaeda had been linked to earlier terrorist plots and actions, including a bomb attack on the World Trade Center in 1993 and one on the U.S naval destroyer *Cole* in 2000. On the morning of 9/11, as soon as Tenet heard about the attacks on the World Trade Center, he had declared, "This has bin Laden all over it."

While the president was transported from Florida to Nebraska, and then to Washington in the evening, Americans saw the horrific events of 9/11 unfold on their televisions. The twin towers of the World Trade Center collapsed amid clouds of smoke and debris. Fireballs engulfed part of the Pentagon. Nearly three thousand people were killed as a result of the hijackings and the attacks. Across the country, worried travelers thronged airports, unable to reach their destinations because all air traffic had been grounded.

The full human and economic scope of 9/11 would not be known for days, weeks, even months. During that first long day, however, President Bush went before television cameras twice to reassure the American people. The first time was in Florida, soon after the president left the Sarasota schoolroom. That night, after returning to Washington, he made a speech that was broadcast from his office in the West Wing of the White House. Bush told Americans that their government was responding to "a series of deliberate and deadly terrorist acts." He declared, "The search is underway for those who are behind these evil acts. I've directed the full resources of our intelligence and law enforcement communities to find those responsible and to bring them to justice. We will make no distinction between the terrorists who committed these acts and those who harbor them."

PEARL HARBOR OF THE TWENTY-FIRST CENTURY

One of President Bush's last acts on 9/11 was to make a brief note in his daily diary. "The Pearl Harbor of the 21st century took place today," he wrote. "We think it's Osama bin

Laden. We think there are other targets in the United States, but I have urged the country to go back to normal. We cannot allow a terrorist thug to hold us hostage. My hope is that this will provide an opportunity for us to rally the world against terrorism."

"Pearl Harbor" was a reference to the Japanese attack on American naval ships that were docked at Pearl Harbor, Hawaii, in 1941. That fateful attack drew the United States into World War II, pitting American troops against the armed forces of enemy nations in Europe and the Pacific. Bush's "Pearl Harbor of the 21st century," the 9/11 terrorist attacks, would also draw the United States into war—a conflict that the Bush administration named the war on terror.

The war on terror would be fought militarily, first in Afghanistan and later in Iraq, two Muslim nations with factions that supported or were believed to support Al-Qaeda. But the war on terror would be fought in the halls of Congress and in U.S. courtrooms as well as on foreign battlefields. As Americans looked to their government for protection from further attacks, the nation's lawmakers would hasten to create new antiterrorist legislation. In time, the court system would weigh and test the new laws.

FIGHTING TERRORISM

Many of the government leaders who made public statements on 9/11 promised action against terrorism. One was Senator Tom Daschle of South Dakota. Daschle was the Senate majority leader. The senators belonging to the political party that controlled the majority of Senate seats—which happened to be the Democratic Party in 2001—had chosen him as their spokesperson. Daschle responded to the terrorist attacks on New York City and Washington with a statement in which he pledged that the nation's lawmakers were determined to avenge the attacks:

> Congress will convene tomorrow. And we will speak with one voice to condemn these attacks, to comfort the victims and their families, to commit our full support to the effort to bring those responsible to justice.
>
> We, Republicans and Democrats, House and Senate, stand strongly behind the president, and we'll work together to ensure that the full resources of the government are brought to bear in these efforts.

Daschle's statement reflected the spirit of unity that gripped the United States in the wake of the attacks. Republicans and Democrats, conservatives and liberals, Americans of all political viewpoints felt an upsurge of patriotism. The country saw an outpouring of sympathy and aid for the victims of the attacks and their families, along with a rising tide of anger toward those who had inspired, planned, and carried out the attacks.

Within the government, the two political parties agreed on the urgent necessity of a legislative response to 9/11. Republicans, the more conservative party, were traditionally associated with a desire for stronger law enforcement powers. But Democrats also believed that the American people expected them to pass new laws that would make it easier for the Federal Bureau of Investigation (FBI), the Central Intelligence Agency, and other agencies to combat terrorism. Both parties knew that they would be expected to act quickly, in the hope of preventing more attacks, if any were planned.

The lawmakers in Congress were not the only people thinking about new laws. On the afternoon of 9/11, Viet Dinh and his coworkers at the Justice Department felt outrage, anger, and grief for the death of political commentator Barbara Olson, the wife of a colleague from the Justice Department; she had been one of the passengers aboard the plane that flew into the Pentagon. In the midst of sorrow and shock, however, Dinh and the others also discussed ways of preventing such horrors from happening again. They talked about revising the nation's antiterrorism laws, about legal changes that could provide stronger tools for striking back at terrorists, and about strengthening the nation's protection.

The following morning, Dinh was back in his office at the Department of Justice. Soon he received instructions from Attorney General Ashcroft and relayed them to half a dozen lawyers and advisers on his staff. Their mission was to research and write the draft of a far-reaching legislative package. Echoing Ashcroft's words, Dinh told the group that the legislation should contain "all that is necessary for law enforcement, within the bounds of the Constitution, to discharge the obligation to fight this war against terror." The result would be the Patriot Act.

The Patriot Act has been praised, criticized, reviewed, and revised. During the Bush presidency and later, after Barack Obama took office as president in 2009, provisions of the act have been tested in court cases, some of which have reached the U.S. Supreme Court. Today, its supporters feel that the act remains what its authors intended it to be, America's most powerful legislative weapon against terrorists. To its critics, however, it is also the greatest threat to civil liberties since the Red Scare of the 1940s and 1950s.

Senator Patrick Leahy, Democrat of Vermont, quickly became deeply involved in creating the Senate's version of an antiterrorism bill. The liberal senator was very concerned that people's civil liberties not be compromised under the guise of protecting the nation from harm.

CHAPTER TWO

A Need for a New Law

Viet Dinh threw himself into the task of writing a new antiterrorism law. Several times during the following week the assistant attorney general worked late into the night, with just a few hours' sleep on a couch in his office. By September 15, four days after the terrorist attacks, the Justice Department staff was able to present Attorney General Ashcroft with a draft of the proposed new law.

On that day Ashcroft and the rest of the Cabinet met with President Bush and his staff at Camp David, the presidential retreat in Maryland, for an all-day summit to discuss terrorism. Each member of the Cabinet spoke in turn. Ashcroft was one of the last to speak. He said:

> It is important to disrupt the terrorists right now, and in the immediate future, but we need to remember these are patient people. They waited eight years between their aggressive attacks on our homeland [between the first World Trade Center

bombing in 1993 and the 9/11 attack in 2001]. We need a long-term strategy for dealing with terrorism abroad, and a continuous, long-term program to go after terrorists in our own country, because that's the kind of strategy that they have in place.

When someone asked Ashcroft, "What do you suggest?" he produced his notes on the new antiterrorism law that Dinh and others had been drafting. It was clear that the Justice Department did not intend merely to make suggestions to congressional lawmakers. The department was writing the law it wanted Congress to pass. This, however, was nothing new. Most bills are written by members of Congress, but an outside agency, such as the Justice Department or a lobby representing an industry or other concerned parties, may draft a bill which one or more members of Congress will then sponsor, or introduce to the House of Representatives and the Senate.

CONGRESS TAKES ACTION

While the Justice Department team was writing its proposed antiterrorism law, members of Congress in both the Senate and the House of Representatives were also drafting proposals for new antiterrorism legislation. Again, this was nothing new. It is not uncommon for both chambers of Congress to draw up bills dealing with the same issue. The outcome depends upon which version receives the greatest support from Congress and the White House. Often the final bill combines elements of several proposals.

One senator who was deeply involved in the legislative response to 9/11 was Patrick Leahy, a Democrat from Vermont. Leahy had been at a meeting in the Supreme Court building in Washington when one of the hijacked planes struck the Pentagon on 9/11. He heard the explosion and saw the smoke. That afternoon Leahy watched a military jet cut through the air above the capital. "I was just thinking," he recalled later, "about how angry I was."

Leahy realized immediately that one result of the day's events would be a call for new antiterrorism laws. Leahy was a leader among the nation's lawmakers because he was the chairman of the Senate Judiciary Committee. In addition to holding hearings at which senators examine the candidates nominated by the president to serve as federal judges or Supreme Court justices, the Judiciary Committee reviews proposed new legislative bills that deal with constitutional amendments or with federal criminal law. Before such a bill can go to the full Senate for debate, amendments (additions or changes), and a vote, it must be approved by the Judiciary Committee.

Just two days after the attacks, eight Republican and Democratic senators introduced the Combating Terrorism Act of 2001 to the Senate as an amendment to a budget bill. The Combating Terrorism Act would have allowed the FBI to wiretap telephone and Internet communications, and to collect information about telephone and Internet use, without first obtaining permission from a court as required by earlier laws. The sponsors of the amendment felt that in order for a new antiterrorism law to be effective, it must give the FBI and the Central Intelligence Agency the ability to learn about potential terrorist strikes as early as possible. If agents did not have to request permission before monitoring private communications, they could act faster, perhaps preventing attacks rather than responding to them after they happened.

The contents of the Combating Terrorism Act were not new.

Its proposals had been discussed in Washington for years. Law enforcement officials had strongly supported these proposals, claiming a need for greater freedom and flexibility in monitoring criminal activities in the era of the Internet, cell phones, and cyberspace. Opposition to the proposals had come from members of Congress and others who felt that giving the government uncontrolled power to monitor suspects' communications could too easily lead to violations of people's constitutionally protected civil rights. When the Combating Terrorism Act was presented on the Senate floor, both supporters and critics spoke up.

Orrin Hatch, a Republican senator from Utah who was one of the bill's sponsors, pointed to the devastation caused by the attacks two days earlier when he said, "It is essential that we give our law enforcement authorities every possible tool to search out and bring to justice those individuals who have brought such indiscriminate death into our backyard." Republican Jon Kyl of Arizona, another sponsor, reminded the Senate that the Federal Bureau of Investigation had been asking for expanded surveillance powers for years: "These are the kinds of things that law enforcement has asked us for. This combination is relatively modest in comparison with the kind of terrorist attack we have just suffered."

Hatch's and Kyl's statements echoed the widely held view that nothing mattered more than finding those who had been behind 9/11 and keeping them from launching another terrorist attack on Americans. There were even hints that if the FBI had already been given broader surveillance powers, 9/11 might have been prevented. With the nation still reeling from the tragedy of that day, many Americans held the view that people who had nothing to hide had nothing to fear from increased government surveillance.

Yet some senators were disturbed by provisions of the Combating Terrorism Act. One of them was Patrick Leahy. As a liberal senator who had long been recognized as one of the Senate's strongest supporters of civil rights, he feared that the country's lawmakers were rushing ahead without sufficient thought and discussion.

Addressing his fellow senators, Leahy argued that while protecting the United States from terrorism was indeed an urgent task, protecting the Constitution and the Bill of Rights was also vitally important. He urged his colleagues to proceed with caution in crafting antiterrorism legislation. Leahy also expressed the fear that the terrorist attack would lead to unnecessary surveillance of ordinary citizens: "Maybe the Senate wants to just go ahead and adopt new abilities to wiretap our citizens. Maybe they want to adopt new abilities to go into people's computers. Maybe that will make us feel safer. Maybe. And maybe what the terrorists have done made us a little bit less safe. Maybe they have increased Big Brother in this country."

"Big Brother" was a reference to British writer George Orwell's novel *1984*, which was published in 1949. In Orwell's bleak view of the future, a monstrous, all-powerful government called Big Brother spies on every minute of its citizens' lives in the name of security and order. Yet this extreme vision of the abuse of government power seemed, in September 2001, much less fearsome than the possibility of more American buildings, or whole cities, being reduced to smoking rubble. The Senate unanimously approved the Combating Terrorism Act.

A week later a bill was introduced into the House of Representatives that gave law enforcement broad new powers to track computer users' online activities. Another Senate bill, proposed in late September, changed the way the nation's law enforcement agencies handled foreign intelligence—specifically, information about suspected terrorist activity abroad. These bills were never signed into law, and neither was the Combating Terrorism Act of 2001, because the key points of all three were incorporated into the other, more comprehensive antiterrorism bills that were being developed at the same time in the Justice Department and Congress.

CONCERNS ABOUT CIVIL LIBERTIES

Leahy, together with colleagues and staff members, worked on the Senate's version of a new antiterrorism law. Leahy's attitude toward the work was shaped by what he saw in the faces of people around him in the days after 9/11. People in Washington wore an expression that Leahy recognized. He had seen it in 1963, when he was a law student, right after an assassin killed President John F. Kennedy. As Leahy explained to a reporter in 2002, "I saw the same shock [after 9/11], and I wanted to make sure our shock didn't turn into panic."

The new antiterrorism law, in Leahy's view, should strike a balance between giving the government more power to look into people's lives and communications, on one hand, and protecting people's privacy and civil liberties on the other. Although Leahy recognized the need for speedy action, he wanted the law to be a thoughtfully crafted piece of legislation, not what he feared would be "a knee-jerk reaction."

Senator Leahy was not the only person who was worried about safeguarding civil liberties in the aftermath of 9/11. The mood of the nation was angry, anxious, and fearful. Some observers felt that the temper of the times tilted so strongly toward security and vengeance that questions of constitutional rights could easily be overlooked.

Worries mounted among civil libertarians—the people and organizations that act as watchdogs for civil liberties and privacy rights. Groups such as the American Civil Liberties Union, the Center for Democracy and Technology, and the Electronic Privacy Information Center had long been concerned about so-called domestic surveillance, which means federal agencies such as the FBI spying on Americans. Now, after 9/11, civil libertarians feared that the government would gain even broader powers of domestic surveillance, powers that could undermine citizens' freedoms without necessarily protecting people from terrorism.

One of those worried civil libertarians was Morton Halperin, a former head of the Washington, D.C., office of the American Civil Liberties Union. Halperin had served as a national security adviser in the Lyndon Johnson, Richard Nixon, and Bill Clinton presidential administrations. On the day after 9/11 he wrote an e-mail to other civil libertarians. It began: "There can be no doubt that we will hear calls in the next few days for congress to enact sweeping legislation to deal with terrorism. This will include . . . broad authority to conduct electronic and other surveillance and to investigate political groups." Halperin sent his e-mail to civil libertarians around the country, saying that it was vitally important to demand protection for civil liberties while the new legislation was being created. "We should not wait," he declared.

The response was immediate. Representatives from the Center for Democracy and Technology and the Electronic Privacy Information Center joined Halperin in writing a proposal that they titled "In Defense of Freedom at a Time of Crisis." A few days after 9/11, people gathered at the national headquarters of the American Civil Liberties Union in Washington to hammer out the final wording of the proposal.

Said Laura Murphy, the director of the national office, "I had never seen that kind of turnout in 25 years. I mean, people were worried. They just knew this [9/11] was a recipe for government overreaching."

The men and women who attended the meeting created a statement that expressed sympathy for victims of the 9/11 attacks and also presented ten points to be considered by lawmakers. The tenth point was this: "We must have faith in our democratic system and our Constitution, and in our ability to protect at the same time both the freedom and the security of all Americans."

Representatives of more than 150 organizations, along with 300 professors of law, signed the statement. The American Civil Liberties Union published the statement on the Internet, released it to the press, and sent it to members of Congress and other government and public figures. To the dismay of Halperin and the other activists, however, the statement got little attention. The nation was focused elsewhere: on the still-smoldering ruins of the World Trade Center and on the search for information about the suicide pilots and hijackers who had caused the destruction.

The American people feared more attacks, possibly with chemical, biological, or even nuclear weapons. Attorney General Ashcroft held a press conference and called on Congress to vote the Justice Department's antiterrorism proposal into law within a week. Senator Leahy noted that Ashcroft's remarks seemed to hint that, as Leahy put it, "we were going to have another attack if we did not agree to this immediately."

A BALANCING ACT
Could Congress and the American public balance the need for rapid action with the need for thoughtful evaluation of

Attorney General John Ashcroft stands in front of some of the photographs of those believed to be the hijackers of the four airplanes that crashed into the World Trade Center, the Pentagon, and Stonycreek Township on September 11, 2001. Ashcroft was a fervent advocate of the Justice Department's antiterrorism law.

the proposed new laws? And would lawmakers be able to balance national security and civil liberties?

When polled soon after 9/11, 61 percent of Americans answered "yes" to the question, "In order to curb terrorism in this country, do you think it will be necessary for the average person to give up some liberties or not?" In the aftermath of the shocking attacks on their country's capital and its largest city, the majority of Americans felt that security from further acts of terrorism should be the nation's top priority. Some possible limitation on privacy or freedom of speech seemed a small price to pay for such security. A close look at the development and passage of the Patriot Act, though, reveals that after 9/11 the country's leaders held differing views on how the United States should respond to the threat of terrorism.

Senators Orrin Hatch (R-UT) and Patrick Leahy (D-VT) attended a hearing in which Attorney General John Ashcroft testified about the need for swift passage of antiterrorist legislation.

CHAPTER THREE

The Path to the Patriot Act

Unlike past wars, the war on terror would not pit U.S. troops against the armed forces of an enemy nation on the battlefield. The war on terror would be, President Bush told the public four days after the attack, "a different kind of conflict against a different kind of enemy." The 9/11 attacks had made it terrifyingly clear that the United States faced bold, elusive, and determined terrorists who could strike at the heart of the American homeland.

While the U.S. military launched assaults on suspected terrorist camps and hideouts in Afghanistan, and the nation waited anxiously to see whether more terrorist attacks would occur, members of the Justice Department and Congress worked to create a new law that would make America more secure. There was no question that such a law was needed. The question now became, Whose version of the antiterrorism legislation will become law?

NEGOTIATIONS

On September 19, 2001, eight days after the terrorist attacks, members of Congress from both political parties, as well as employees of the Department of Justice, attended a meeting in the Capitol Building. Orrin Hatch and Patrick Leahy were among the senators present. Among those who attended from the House of Representatives were Michigan Democrat John Conyers and Texas Republican Richard Armey, who was the leader of the majority party in the House. White House counsel Alberto Gonzales, a legal adviser to President Bush, represented the administration at the meeting. John Ashcroft and Viet Dinh represented the Justice Department.

Both Leahy and Dinh had completed their drafts of proposed new antiterrorism bills. The purpose of the meeting was to exchange the two versions, compare them, and decide what the final bill should contain. Everyone present quickly realized, however, that the differences between Leahy's 165-page proposal and Dinh's forty-page proposal concerned more than length.

Both versions gave new powers to the government, or expanded existing ones. The Justice Department's proposal, however, gave the government significantly more authority to act without supervision, review by the courts, or warrants. It allowed the various branches and agencies of the government, including the Treasury Department, the FBI, and the Central Intelligence Agency, to share information without restrictions. (Rules limiting such information sharing had been created to prevent abuses, as had happened in the past when data gathered by intelligence agencies had been used to harass citizens, or had been improperly applied to criminal investigations.) The Justice Department proposal also authorized Internet service providers to give the FBI access to their customers' e-mail accounts. Overall, this proposed legislation would make it much easier for law enforcement to carry out wiretapping and other surveillance activities.

Leahy was concerned about the broad scope of the Justice Department proposal. After the meeting, he sought a compromise, one that he believed would preserve terrorist-fighting muscle while adding some safeguards for civil liberties and privacy. Leahy and Senate staffers, in communication with members of the Justice Department, developed a compromise bill that included elements from both of the earlier proposals.

One key feature of the compromise was a provision that a court would have to review the sharing of information between intelligence and law enforcement agencies. This process, called judicial review, was an important safeguard. It would not only filter out unnecessary information sharing (and thus reduce the possibility that shared information would be wrongly used), but it would also create a record of what information was shared, and by whom. Another provision of the compromise bill stated that evidence that had been illegally obtained could not be used against U.S. citizens.

During the negotiations to develop the compromise version of the bill, Attorney General Ashcroft was represented by Timothy Flanigan, a Justice Department counsel, or lawyer. On September 30, Flanigan told Leahy that the department had accepted the compromise. Several days later Ashcroft came to Leahy's office for a meeting. Leahy expected the attorney general to finalize his acceptance of the compromise bill, but instead Ashcroft told Leahy that the Justice Department could not accept the compromise.

According to one senator, Democrat Russ Feingold of Wisconsin, the attorney general himself had not turned against the compromise, but President Bush and others in his administration had refused to accept it. No one in the administration explained why the compromise bill had been rejected. News reports at the time suggested that the Bush administration opposed the part of the bill that required a court order before the FBI could share information with other agencies.

THE ORIGINAL PATRIOT ACT

In early October the nation's lawmakers felt increased pressure from the public and the Bush administration to produce an antiterrorism law. Soon after Ashcroft met with Leahy to reject the compromise bill, the attorney general told the press, "I think it is time for us to be productive on behalf of the American people. Talk won't prevent terrorism." Senator Orrin Hatch of Utah, who was also present, added his own criticism of what he regarded as congressional delay: "It's a very dangerous thing. It's time to get off our duffs and do something."

By this time, the House of Representatives was considering the bill that had been developed by its members. So was the Senate. The House's bill was called the Provide Appropriate Tools Required to Intercept and Obstruct Terrorism Act, while the Senate's was the Uniting and Strengthening America Act. The sponsors of each bill had carefully crafted a name that could be shortened into an easy-to-remember, uplifting acronym: the PATRIOT Act and the USA Act. These acronyms also served as a kind of marketing tool, giving each bill a strong, positive "brand name."

The House of Representatives acted first. During the second half of September the House Judiciary Committee— forty-three representatives who were responsible for reviewing proposed new federal criminal laws—had started with the Justice Department's proposal, made some changes and added some new elements, and come up with an antiterrorism bill that was identified in Congressional records as H.R. 2975. This bill was the original PATRIOT Act. It was sponsored by F. James Sensenbrenner Jr. of Wisconsin, a Republican, and twenty-two other representatives, both Republicans and Democrats. The bill reined in some of the new powers that the Justice Department had proposed. In *The Patriot Act: A Documentary and Reference Guide* (2007), Herbert N. Foerstel calls H.R. 2975 "a more balanced Patriot Act bill, providing new national security authorities without sacrificing fundamental civil liberties."

One of the House Judiciary Committee's most important additions to the antiterrorism bill was a "sunset" provision suggested by Richard Armey, the Texas Republican who was House majority leader. Under the sunset provision, sixteen sections of the law would expire in four years unless renewed by Congress. This measure ensured that the parts of the law that worried civil libertarians, such as investigators' power to place wiretaps on many phones using only one warrant, would either disappear or come under congressional review.

On October 3 the House Judiciary Committee voted on H.R. 2975. All forty-three members of the committee approved the bill. Its next step would be a vote by the entire House of Representatives.

"THE CLOCK IS TICKING"

The Senate's antiterrorism bill, meanwhile, had bypassed a formal review by the Senate Judiciary Committee. Senators Leahy, Hatch, and other committee members had agreed to work with the Department of Justice to draft a bill that could go straight to the entire Senate for a vote. The resulting bill,

S. 1510 or the USA Act, was closely based on the proposal written by Dinh and the Justice Department. The senators had made some amendments to the text, but S. 1510 contained fewer changes than the earlier, rejected compromise bill had contained.

S. 1510, sponsored by Democrat Tom Daschle of South Dakota and six other senators, came before the Senate for debate and a vote on October 11. Senate majority leader Daschle urged his fellow senators to accept the bill without delay and without amendments. Several senators, however, raised cautionary voices. One of them was Republican Arlen Specter of Pennsylvania. Specter warned that if the Senate passed the bill without sufficient consideration and debate, the Supreme Court might later overturn the bill as unconstitutional.

Wisconsin Senator Feingold, a Democrat, did not want to let the USA Act pass without offering some amendments to protect civil liberties. In Feingold's view, preserving the freedoms that make up the foundation of American life was as important as protecting the nation from terrorism. His address to the Senate included these words:

> There is no doubt that if we lived in a police state, it would be easier to catch terrorists. If we lived in a country where the police were allowed to search your home at any time for any reason; if we lived in a country where the government was entitled to open your mail, eavesdrop on your phone conversations, or intercept your e-mail communications; if we lived in a country where people could be held in jail indefinitely based on what they write or think, or based on mere suspicion that they were up to no good, the government would probably

discover and arrest more terrorists, or would-be terrorists, just as it would find more lawbreakers generally. But that would not be a country in which we would want to live, and it would not be a country for which we could, in good conscience, ask our young people to fight and die. In short, that country would not be America.

Feingold went on to remind the senators that the Constitution and the Bill of Rights had been written "to protect individual liberties in times of war as well as in times of peace." He then introduced the first of three amendments he thought the Senate should consider before voting on the USA Act.

A few minutes later Daschle took the floor. He mentioned "the very delicate balance between civil liberties and law enforcement that we had to achieve in bringing a bill of this complexity to the floor" and again urged the senators to act quickly and without further debate. "We have a job to do," he told them. "The clock is ticking. The work needs to get done. . . . Let's move on and finish this bill." Daschle asked the senators to table, or set aside, Feingold's proposed amendment to the act.

Senator Leahy, who had earlier fought to amend the Justice Department proposal, also called on his fellow senators to pass S. 1510 without amendments. He said that he agreed with the substance of Feingold's amendment—in fact, he would have liked to go even further in modifying the bill. But he added, "I can tell you right now, if we start unraveling this bill, we are going to lose all the parts we won and we will be back to a proposal that was blatantly unconstitutional in many parts."

In the end, the Senate voted to table all three of Feingold's proposed amendments. It was, Feingold later recalled, "a low point for me in terms of being a Democrat and somebody who believes in civil liberties." At 11:43 p.m. the Senate voted on S. 1510. Three senators did not vote. Ninety-six senators voted yes. Russ Feingold voted no. The bill was passed.

THE USA PATRIOT ACT

On October 12, the day after the Senate passed the USA Act, the House of Representatives voted on H.R. 2975, the PATRIOT Act. Little more than a week earlier, the House Judiciary Committee had unanimously voted in favor of the act. When the act was put to a vote by the entire House, however, the results were not unanimous.

Conyers was one of seventy-nine representatives who voted no on H.R. 2975—yet he had been one of the sponsors who introduced the bill to the House Judiciary Committee. Why would Conyers vote against a bill that he had sponsored? In a 2002 interview he explained his change of position, saying, "What you need to know is that the Patriot Act that I sponsored is not the Patriot Act that was passed."

When members of the House met on October 12 to vote on H.R. 2975, they recognized that the text of the bill before them was not the text that the House Judiciary Committee had passed. Congresswoman Louise Slaughter, a Democrat from New York and a member of the House Committee on Rules, described the situation to her fellow representatives:

> While the Committee on the Judiciary had reported a truly bipartisan bill by a vote of 36-0, which is somewhat miraculous, 2 weeks ago, we were not informed until 7 o'clock this morning that we would be taking testimony on a new bill, the

content of which the Committee on Rules had not seen nor apparently had the members of the Committee on the Judiciary.

The language of the original Patriot Act had been replaced by language more like that of the just-passed Senate bill, which more closely resembled the Justice Department's initial proposal. According to Representative Conyers, House leaders had been influenced by the Bush administration and Attorney General Ashcroft to change the text of the bill. In remarks that were read into the Congressional Record, Conyers said, "What we have before us is a tale of two bills. One bill was crafted by the standing committee of the House. The other was crafted by the Attorney General and the President." The bill that came before the House of Representatives for a vote on October 12 was, says Conyers, "a bill that was foreign to all of us on the Committee."

In Conyers's view, the Judiciary Committee's original version of the bill "did not ignore constitutional questions the way the present [new] Patriot Act did." The new version of the bill did, however, preserve Representative Armey's sunset provision, which meant that some parts of the law would expire in four years unless Congress renewed them.

Most of the representatives in the House had not had time to read the new version of H.R. 2975, because it had been delivered to them only that morning. Still, support for the revised bill was strong. Peter Deutsch, a Democratic representative from Florida, urged his colleagues to pass it. Deutsch felt that the Judiciary Committee's version of the bill had had "some very, very specific problems," and he agreed with President Bush that the nation was at war and needed strong tools to defend itself against terrorism. Many members of the House of Representatives shared Deutsch's view. When the vote was held, H.R. 2975 passed by 337 to 79.

At this point the Senate and the House of Representatives had each approved an antiterrorism bill. Now the judiciary committees of both chambers had to merge the two bills into a single bill. The House and Senate would vote again on the unified bill before it could become law.

The merging of the two bills produced the Uniting and Strengthening America by Providing Appropriate Tools Required to Intercept and Obstruct Terrorism Act of 2001— also known as the USA PATRIOT Act. It combined elements of the Senate's USA bill, S. 1510, and the House's PATRIOT bill, H.R. 2975 (including the sunset provision). It also contained some parts of another recently proposed law, the Financial Anti-Terrorism Act, or H.R. 3004.

On October 23 Sensenbrenner introduced the USA PATRIOT Act to the House of Representatives as H.R. 3162. The next day the House passed the bill by a vote of 357 to 66. The following day the Senate met to consider the bill. In his role as chairman of the Judiciary Committee, Leahy told his fellow senators, "Senate passage of this measure without amendment will amount to final passage of this important legislation, and the bill will be sent to the President for his signature."

Leahy admitted that the USA PATRIOT Act fell short of his vision of the ideal antiterrorism law. He said, "This was not the bill that I, or any of the sponsors, would have written if compromise was unnecessary. . . . In negotiations with the Administration, I did my best to strike a reasonable balance between the need to address the threat of terrorism, which we all keenly feel today, and the need to protect our constitutional freedoms. Despite my misgivings, I acquiesced in [accepted] some of the Administration's proposals to move the legislative process forward." Leahy also reminded his listeners that no law could ensure complete security: "No one can guarantee that Americans will be free from the threat of future terrorist attacks, and to suggest that this legislation— or any legislation—would or could provide such a guarantee would be a false promise of security to the public."

Finally, Leahy pointed out that the USA PATRIOT Act, by expanding the government's powers to gather information and to keep watch on citizens, would change many aspects of law enforcement, not just the war on terrorism. He reminded the senators that it would be Congress's duty to remain watchful. The nation's lawmakers would have to keep a close eye on how the Justice Department, the FBI, and the president used their expanded powers. Congress must remain alert for possible abuses of the act.

Despite these cautions, Leahy believed that the process of negotiation and discussion—hasty though it may have been compared with normal congressional procedures—had improved the law that the Justice Department had written right after 9/11. The final version of the USA PATRIOT Act, declared Leahy, was "a far better bill than the Administration proposed" and "a better bill than either the House or the Senate had initially approved."

All that remained was for the Senate to vote. Ninety-eight senators voted to pass the bill. Russ Feingold cast the only vote against it, and Mary Landrieu, a Democrat from Louisiana, did not vote. On the following day, October 26, 2001, President George W. Bush signed the USA PATRIOT Act into law, declaring, "This legislation is essential not only to pursuing and punishing terrorists but also preventing more atrocities in [sic] the hands of the evil ones. This government will enforce this law with all the urgency of a nation at war."

Civil liberties are most likely to be suppressed during times of war. In World War II, Japanese Americans were shorn of their property, rights, and livelihoods and interned at camps such as this one in Manzanar, California, for no reason aside from their ancestry.

CHAPTER FOUR

Balancing Freedom and Security

The USA PATRIOT Act of 2001, generally called simply the Patriot Act, was the American government's response to a shocking attack on the United States and to the threat of twenty-first-century terrorism. Yet the Patriot Act was also part of a long history of debates and decisions concerning the proper balance between national security and individual liberty.

What rights do individual citizens possess, and what powers properly belong to governments? When, and to what extent, should a government's power override the rights of its citizens? English lawmakers considered these matters before the United States was born. Later the American people and their elected leaders wrestled with the same questions, answering them in different ways at different times.

ORIGINS OF MODERN CIVIL LIBERTIES

"Civil liberties" is a general term for the rights and freedoms of citizens in a state ruled by law. Exactly what those rights and freedoms *are* varies from one country to another, and so does the extent to which the government protects or enforces them. Americans today take well-deserved pride in their civil liberties, which are a cornerstone of the nation's legal system. Yet the civil liberties that are known and cherished in the United States are not a purely American invention. Although America's civil liberties have been defined and expanded over the course of U.S. history by the country's courts and legislatures, they originated in a centuries-old tradition of English law and in a European philosophical movement.

One of the first steps toward modern civil liberties was made by King John of England in 1215. It was a reluctant step. The king was prodded forward, so to speak, by swords leveled at his back.

An army of John's subjects, infuriated by what they regarded as excessive taxation to pay for wars he had waged in France, marched against the king and demanded that he sign a document in which he accepted limitations on royal power. To keep his throne, John signed it. That document, known as the Magna Carta, required the king to get the approval of various groups, such as the church and the nobles, before imposing certain kinds of taxes. It also prevented the king from doing away with jury trials and from abusing royal privileges. Yet more important than any particular provision of the Magna Carta was the principle that the agreement represented. A monarch could not rule by whim or will alone but must submit to certain limitations. Kings were no longer above the law—at least in England.

The Magna Carta was soon followed by the birth of Parliament, England's body of elected representatives. At first Parliament served mainly as a mouthpiece for the monarch, who freely ignored or dismissed the elected assembly. The power of Parliament gradually widened as its members advised, negotiated with, and even opposed England's rulers. By the middle of the seventeenth century, Parliament was strong enough to dismiss an unpopular king, James II, and offer the throne to his son-in-law and daughter, William and Mary. This shift in power became known as the Glorious Revolution, and it was a revolutionary transformation. After the Glorious Revolution, William and Mary ruled as monarchs, but the true power of governing the country lay with Parliament.

In 1689 England's new monarchs willingly agreed to a Bill of Rights that guaranteed certain freedoms and rights to their subjects. Among these were freedom from cruel and unusual punishment and the right to elect parliamentary representatives without the interference of the monarch. By the time Parliament presented the bill to William and Mary, English colonies had already taken root in North America. During the following century the English Bill of Rights would influence political thinkers there.

The year that saw England's dual monarchs accept the Bill of Rights also saw the first appearance of a book destined to shape people's ideas about civil liberties in England, the English colonies, and beyond. That book was *Two Treatises of Government.* Although at first the book was published anonymously, its author was an English philosopher and political thinker named John Locke. He gave the book's second section the subtitle "An Essay Concerning the True Original Extent and End of Civil Government." Today this part of Locke's book is generally called "The Second Treatise of Civil Government." It sets forth Locke's views on how and why people organize themselves into states under governments, on the proper role of governments, and on the limits of governments' powers.

People are naturally free, Locke argued, but complete freedom for all quickly turns to anarchy, a violent and uncertain existence in which the strong can prey upon the weak. To achieve a measure of stability and security, people band together into societies "for the mutual preservation of their lives, liberties and estates." Individuals give up a certain measure of freedom, in other words, in exchange for security.

Locke regarded the relationship between the people of a society and their government as a contract, in which each side has rights and responsibilities. The people give to their government certain powers, such as the power to make laws and impose taxes, but in turn the government bears the responsibility of protecting the people and ruling according to law. Citizens, on their side, have certain rights, such as those guaranteed by the English Bill of Rights, but they also have responsibilities, such as obeying the laws and paying their taxes.

The views that Locke expressed in *Two Treatises of Government* were part of an intellectual and cultural movement that arose in Europe in the late seventeenth century and flourished through the eighteenth century. This movement is now known as the Enlightenment. It was fueled by writings from philosophers, scholars, and scientists in France, Scotland, Germany, Italy, and England, and it celebrated the power of reason. Enlightenment thinkers believed that knowledge and rational thought were the best tools for improving lives, solving social problems, and understanding the world.

Locke was not the only Enlightenment thinker to turn his attention to the question of the proper relations between rulers and the ruled. Although the writers who explored political philosophy had differing ideas about the best way to organize a state or run a government, many of them shared Locke's view that a society exists through a type of contract between people and their government. As that notion took hold, it had important results in the North American colonies that would become the United States.

QUESTIONS OF CONSTITUTIONALITY

An edition of Locke's second treatise was published in the American colonies in 1773, at a time when relations between the colonies and England were tense and nearing the breaking point. Some of the colonial leaders and thinkers who are now remembered as founders of the nation, including Samuel Adams and Thomas Jefferson, read Locke and greeted his ideas with enthusiasm.

A few years later, Jefferson sat down to write the Declaration of Independence. The opening sentence carries a clear echo of Locke in the claim that a "separate and equal station" is the natural position of all people. In the following paragraph, in discussing what he called "unalienable Rights," Jefferson set forth points that he called "self-evident," or obvious: that people are created equal and that they have rights that cannot be taken away. Those rights include "Life, Liberty, and the pursuit of Happiness." The Declaration goes on to state that "to secure these rights, Governments are instituted among Men, deriving their just powers from the consent of the governed." From the very start, American political thought rested on the principle that governments exist by the will of the people, and that both those who govern and those who are governed have certain rights and responsibilities.

Once the North American colonies had won their independence, the newly created United States embodied the founders' ideas about government in the Constitution, which each colony eventually ratified, or accepted as law. Yet when the Constitution went into effect in 1788 it lacked specific protections for individual rights and freedoms. That problem was corrected in 1791 by the first ten amendments to the Constitution. Together the first through tenth amendments are known as the Bill of Rights. Some of them were modeled on the English Bill of Rights of 1689, even to the point of using the same wording.

The Bill of Rights guarantees that Americans possess certain liberties. They may speak freely, for example, and operate a free press, and assemble for any purpose as long as the assembly is peaceful. Certain amendments have played a role in debates and legal challenges concerning issues of privacy, civil liberties, and security. One is the Fourth Amendment, which guarantees "the right of the people to be secure in their persons, houses, papers, and effects, against unreasonable searches and seizures." The Fourth Amendment does *not* say that people may not be searched or arrested. It says that searches and seizures may not be "unreasonable," meaning that there must be good grounds for such actions by the government against its citizens. The Ninth Amendment says that the fact that specific rights are listed in the Constitution and its amendments does not mean that the people have only those rights and no others.

Another constitutional amendment figures in many current cases involving freedom and law enforcement. Passed in 1868, the Fourteenth Amendment was concerned with issues that arose in the aftermath of the Civil War, including the rights of freed slaves in Southern states and the question of whether people who had fought against the Union could hold public office. The first section of the amendment, however, contains a statement with broad significance. Its wording echoes both Locke's Second Treatise and the Declaration of Independence:

No State shall make or enforce any law which shall abridge [reduce] the privileges or immunities [rights or freedoms] of citizens of the United States; nor shall any State deprive any person of life, liberty, or property without due process of law; nor deny to any person within its jurisdiction the equal protection of the laws.

The importance of the Fourteenth Amendment lies in the way it has been interpreted over the years. The principal interpreter has been the U.S. Supreme Court.

The Supreme Court's power to interpret the Constitution was established decades before the Fourteenth Amendment came into existence. That power dates from 1803, when the Supreme Court heard a case called *Marbury* v. *Madison.* In their decision on that case, the justices of the Court struck down, or did away with, a law that they determined violated the Constitution. *Marbury* v. *Madison* established the Supreme Court's authority to overturn legislation that it finds to be unconstitutional, and since that time the Court has been the final interpreter of the Constitution. The justices of the Court have the last word on whether a law is or is not constitutional.

Several twentieth-century Supreme Court cases had particular importance to the development and protection of civil rights. *Gitlow* v. *New York* (1925) established the principle that the Fourteenth Amendment, which guarantees equal treatment under the law, requires all states to extend the protections of the Bill of Rights to all citizens. In *Brown* v. *Board of Education of Topeka* (1954), the Court ruled that segregating, or separating, schoolchildren by race was unlawful because it violated the Fourteenth Amendment. Eleven years later, in *Griswold* v. *Connecticut,* the Court determined that the Fourth,

Ninth, and Fourteenth Amendments together create a right to privacy. The *Griswold* case established that, even though the word "privacy" appears nowhere in the Constitution or its amendments, individual privacy is nonetheless constitutionally protected. Since that time, many legal disputes over civil liberties have focused on such questions as how *much* privacy the Constitution grants, and when and under what circumstances the state's interests override those rights.

CONFLICTING INTERESTS

"Silent enim leges inter arma," declared the Roman orator Marcus Tullius Cicero in the first century BCE. Cicero's statement is generally translated from Latin as "In times of war, laws are silent." It refers to the fact that war—or even the threat of war—can override all else. When nations or governments are at war, or fear they will soon come under attack, they may suspend normal laws or redefine people's rights in the name of security.

"Security," in such cases, can mean more than fighting an enemy force or patrolling a nation's borders. It can also refer to maintaining internal order; to combating espionage; to banning the publication of certain kinds of articles or books; and to directing the use of resources toward the war effort through such means as rationing food, shifting industrial production from cars to tanks, or requiring citizens to serve in the armed forces.

Cicero's observation has been proven true many times in many nations, including several episodes in modern American history. In April 1917 the United States entered World War I, which had been raging in Europe since 1914. Two months later Congress passed the Espionage Act, which established stern punishments for spying, for promoting the success of the enemy, and for interfering with U.S. military operations, including recruiting for the armed forces.

The provisions of the Espionage Act of 1917 appear to be reasonable precautions for any nation at war. Espionage and treason are very serious offenses that have historically carried grave penalties. In practice, however, governments and law enforcement can stretch concepts such as "promoting the success of the enemy" and "preventing interference with recruiting" to cover a broad range of activities. Someone who criticizes the war or the way a particular aspect of the war is being handled, or who expresses sympathy for civilians killed on the enemy side, may be accused of undermining the war effort or aiding the enemy's cause. So may someone who practices or advocates pacifism, the refusal to fight based on religious or philosophical beliefs.

In 1918 Congress passed the Sedition Act, which expanded the scope of the Espionage Act by making it a crime to print or speak anything disloyal, scornful, or abusive about, or even to ridicule, the U.S. government, Constitution, flag, armed forces, or military uniforms. Acting under the Espionage and Sedition acts, federal and state officials shut down newspapers and magazines that they considered unpatriotic, dangerous, or un-American.

The chief target of these laws was not Germany, America's main opponent in World War I. Instead, the laws were aimed at certain people within the United States, particularly people who were associated with two movements that had originated in Europe in the nineteenth century. One of those movements was socialism, a system of social and economic organization that gives ownership of the means of economic production, such as farms and factories, to the community or state rather than to private individuals. The other movement grew out of a political philosophy called anarchism. Although anarchism has taken many forms, at its most basic it calls for the end of compulsory government, or any form of government to which people are required to submit.

Socialism's insistence that workers should share the power held by business owners, and anarchism's scorn for authority, were profoundly threatening to many Americans in the early twentieth century. Prominent socialist and anarchist leaders, as well as many members of the movements, were immigrants from Russia, Poland, Italy, or other European nations. For this reason Americans began to view immigrants in general as dangerous and untrustworthy. An immigration law passed in 1918 gave the federal government the power to turn away immigrants who were anarchists. The law also allowed federal officials to deport, or send back to their country of origin, foreign-born anarchists who were living in the United States.

Alarm about political activism in the United States was fueled by events in Russia, where a revolution in 1917 had toppled the centuries-old monarchy and created a new communist government. Under communism, an outgrowth of socialism, Russia was renamed the Soviet Union and reorganized into a one-party political system with a state-controlled economy.

Americans worried that Reds—as socialists and communists have been called—might be planning a similar revolution in the United States. Although such an outcome was never likely, socialists *were* involved in the American labor movement. Strikes by that movement had led to bitter fighting at factories and mines when workers refused to allow production to continue until business owners met their demands for better pay or working conditions. Furthermore, some activists, especially among the anarchists, believed it was right to use any means, including violence, to bring about change or to overthrow a government. Many of these individuals limited their activities to making speeches and writing pamphlets, but some put their beliefs into action, usually by making bombs or attempting to assassinate public figures.

World War I ended in 1918, but domestic trouble continued. June 1919 saw a particularly severe outbreak of anarchist bombings. Explosions occurred in eight cities. In Washington, D.C., a bomb exploded outside the house of A. Mitchell Palmer, the newly appointed attorney general of the United States. Palmer was already a vigorous foe of socialism and anarchism, forces that he would describe, one year later, as intent on destroying America:

> Like a prairie-fire, the blaze of revolution was sweeping over every American institution of law and order a year ago. It was eating its way into the homes of the American workmen, its sharp tongues of revolutionary heat were licking the altars of the churches, leaping into the belfry of the school bell, crawling into the sacred corners of American homes, seeking to replace marriage vows with libertine laws, burning up the foundations of society.

The wave of bombings increased Palmer's determination to end this menace. With the help of the Immigration and Naturalization Service and a young Justice Department official named J. Edgar Hoover, the attorney general launched a series of raids against labor union headquarters, the offices of socialist and communist groups, and the homes and haunts of suspected anarchists. Beginning in November 1919, federal agents rounded up thousands of people in these raids. Some were tried for specific crimes. Others were simply held without trial for varying periods of time. Hundreds were deported.

The Palmer Raids, as they came to be called, continued through June 1920. Public support of the raids declined after several judges and legal scholars—including Felix Frankfurter, an Austrian-born immigrant who would later become a justice of the Supreme Court—criticized them as violations of the free speech rights guaranteed by the Bill of Rights.

In a history of free speech in the United States, civil libertarian Christopher M. Finan writes, "The people who were arrested during the Palmer Raids were picked up not because of anything they had done but because of what they might do. In fact, many of those arrested and held for deportation did not believe in violence. . . . But the government raids did achieve something important. They raised the issue of what freedoms are protected by the First Amendment to the U.S. Constitution." In a time of war and unrest, fear and the wish to keep order had temporarily quelled freedom of belief and speech.

MORE WARS, MORE SCARES

The laws of civil liberty again fell silent during World War II, when the United States went to war with Japan. At that time the U.S. government forced thousands of Japanese Americans, many of them U.S.-born citizens, to leave their homes and businesses so that they could spend the war under guard in camps called internment centers, even though they had not been convicted or even accused of specific crimes.

Japanese Americans were interned solely on the basis of their racial and ethnic identity, because the U.S. government—and many of the country's citizens—feared that Americans of Japanese descent would be loyal to Japan instead of to the United States. The internment was an example of ethnic profiling, targeting a particular group of people because it was thought that they *might* pose a threat, not because it had been proven that they did pose one.

After the war ended in 1945, U.S. leaders grew concerned about the Soviet Union's military might, about Soviet control of neighboring countries in Eastern Europe, and about the rise of communism in a number of Asian, African, and Latin American nations. Along with these concerns came growing unease about communism in the United States. The result was a second Red Scare, a period during which people in America—mostly U.S. citizens this time—were penalized for their political beliefs and for what they wrote or said, not for criminal acts. Persecution also occurred even in the absence of evidence about people's political beliefs or thoughts; some were penalized on the basis of unfounded suspicion, or because they were—or were believed to be—homosexual.

Socialist leaders had already been convicted and imprisoned under a 1940 law that made it illegal to belong to an organization that favored the violent overthrow of the U.S. government. Members of the Communist Party of the United States (CPUSA) had escaped that fate during the war years because the CPUSA officially supported the war effort. After the war, however, several highly publicized cases of people accused of spying for the Soviet Union inside the United States fanned anticommunist feeling, and the Red Scare was under way.

"This Sacred

On December 21, 1919, the ship *Buford* made its way through New York Harbor, past the Statue of Liberty. The *Buford*, which belonged to the U.S. government, was bound for port in Finland, but ultimately the prisoners were bound for Russia. Aboard were 249 prisoners, guarded by soldiers. The prisoners were radicals, political activists, and anarchists who were being deported—removed by force from the United States. One of them was fifty-one-year-old Emma Goldman.

Born in 1869 in Lithuania, which was then part of the Russian empire, Goldman had come to the United States at the age of sixteen. Long before the Palmer Raids she was widely known as an anarchist who envisioned a society of complete equality—and who claimed that violence was sometimes necessary as the only way to achieve this goal. In 1917 Goldman was arrested for speaking and writing against U.S. participation in World War I, including urging young men not to register for military service. She served a two-year prison sentence and was then deported. At Goldman's deportation hearing her attorney read her statement, which included these words:

> Ever since I have been in this country—and I have lived here practically all my life—it has been dinned into my ears that under the institutions of this alleged Democracy one is entirely free to think and feel as he pleases. What becomes of this sacred guarantee of freedom of thought and conscience when persons are being persecuted and driven out for the very motives and purposes for which the pioneers who built up this country laid down their lives? . . . Under the mask of the same Anti-Anarchist law every criticism of a corrupt

Guarantee"

administration, every attack on Government abuse, every manifestation of sympathy with the struggle of another country in the pangs of a new birth—in short, every free expression of untrammeled thought may be suppressed utterly, without even the semblance of an unprejudiced hearing or a fair trial. . . . The free expression of the hopes and aspirations of a people is the greatest and only safety in a sane society. In truth, it is such free expression and discussion alone that can point the most beneficial path for human progress and development.

Emma Goldman never returned to the United States. She lived in Russia, England, Canada, France, and Spain until her death in 1940. The U.S. government then allowed her to be buried in Chicago, in a cemetery that holds the remains of other labor activists and political radicals who were active in the early twentieth century.

Current and former members of the Communist Party in the United States were brought before congressional committees. So were people who subscribed to communist or socialist publications, attended meetings, or were simply suspected of being sympathetic to communism. At the congressional hearings they were interrogated about their political beliefs and pressured to identify other communists or sympathizers. Many people in certain industries, such as publishing and moviemaking, were blacklisted, which means that they were prevented from getting work. Investigators examined the backgrounds of federal employees, who were fired at the slightest hint of possible disloyalty.

The Red Scare died down in the late 1950s. People began to see the relentless hunt for communists and the attacks on freedom of thought as too extreme. The anticommunist crusade began to be called a "witch hunt"—a feverish, destructive, and unbalanced search for imaginary enemies, like the Salem witch trials of 1692, a black mark in American colonial history, during which more than 160 people were accused of being witches. Twenty were executed on the basis of "evidence" that was either imagined or fabricated.

Real threats to U.S. security still existed. Yet in the years that followed, agencies that existed to protect Americans from crime and from espionage and other genuine foreign threats also took aim at political dissenters, antiwar protestors, and even the civil rights movement that formed to oppose racial discrimination. Eventually these activities— including abuses of power and violations of civil rights— would prompt the nation's leaders to make major reforms in U.S. law enforcement and intelligence operations. Those reforms, in turn, became the springboard for the Patriot Act.

CHAPTER FIVE

Before the Patriot Act: FISA

"The 9/11 attacks occurred on a Tuesday," writes John Ashcroft in a memoir of his time as the attorney general of the United States. "By Saturday, we had a full-blown legislative proposal. Part of the reason we were able to move so quickly was that a number of the provisions had been proposed to Congress in 1996, and Congress had rejected them. They hadn't wanted to give law enforcement that much power. But after the bloodshed of 9/11, few congressmen did not want to be aggressive in pursuing terrorists."

The Justice Department could quickly write the first draft of what eventually became the Patriot Act because much of the writing had been done already. That fact has been interpreted in different ways. Herbert N. Foerstel, a civil libertarian, shares the critical opinion that the war on terror after 9/11 gave the executive branch of government—the Bush administration and some members of the Justice Department—a chance to gain powers they had wanted for some time, but had been unable to obtain because Congress considered those powers to be unconstitutional. Says Foerstel:

> In reality, the Patriot Act was not a bold new anti-terrorism bill. It was a resurrected wish-list of executive powers that had accumulated in the Justice Department over many years, powers that, when conceived, had little or no relevance to terrorism and which Congress rejected as unnecessary infringements on civil liberties.

Many people in government and law enforcement, however, held precisely the opposite view. If the Patriot Act was a recycled "wish list" of expanded executive powers, that was simply because those powers had been needed for a long time, but Congress and former Justice Department officials had failed to recognize the need. Ashcroft explains:

> In the decades prior to 9/11, the U.S. Congress and Department of Justice officials had designed a system that actually made it more difficult for our nation to protect itself against terrorism. Indeed, it was a tragedy waiting to happen, a system destined to fail. . . . The [Patriot Act] provided our nation's law enforcement, national defense, and intelligence agencies with new or enhanced tools to disrupt, detain, and bring terrorists and other dangerous criminals to justice.

The Patriot Act was a revision and updating of laws and programs that had been on the national books for years, chiefly a 1978 law called the Foreign Intelligence Surveillance Act (FISA). Congress had passed FISA to correct serious problems within the nation's law enforcement and intelligence agencies. At the root of some of those problems was J. Edgar Hoover.

Hoover was the lieutenant of Attorney General A. Mitchell Palmer during Palmer's counterattack on anarchism in 1919. Five years after the Palmer Raids, Hoover was named acting director of the Bureau of Investigation, which was the forerunner of the Federal Bureau of Investigation. Hoover oversaw the formation of the FBI in 1935 and became its first director, a position he held until his death in 1972.

During his decades at the head of the country's top federal law enforcement agency, Hoover made the FBI into one of the world's most modern and successful anticrime forces. His determination to stamp out political dissent remained as strong as during the days of the Palmer Raids, however, and he continued to fear subversion—the overthrow or undermining of government or society. Hoover's eagerness to sniff out potential subversives—people he thought might pose a threat to national order and stability—led him to involve the FBI in improper and illegal domestic espionage.

COINTELPRO

Bank robbers and gangsters of the 1930s were Hoover's first big targets. The fame Hoover won by bringing down headline-grabbing outlaws such as Machine Gun Kelly and John Dillinger allowed him to expand the Bureau of Investigation into the FBI and become its director. In the years that followed, though, he continued to keep a close eye on politically motivated criminals or troublemakers: socialists, communists, and all sorts of radicals, a term that includes people or groups whose views and goals lie far outside the mainstream on either the liberal or the conservative end of the political spectrum.

In 1946 Hoover started making a list of people in the United States whom he considered dangerous or subversive. These individuals had committed no crimes for which they could be prosecuted under the law, but Hoover doubted their loyalty, and he mistrusted their ideas or the organizations to which they belonged. If the nation went to war or encountered some other type of emergency, he thought, the people on his list could not be trusted. They might commit treason, espionage, or sabotage.

The Korean War began in 1950, pitting U.S.-backed South Korea against Soviet-backed North Korea. By that time, Hoover's list consisted of about 12,000 names. Ninety-seven percent of the people on the list were U.S. citizens. Hoover notified President Harry Truman of the existence of the list and suggested that all of the "potentially dangerous" individuals be rounded up and held in military prisons. Under this plan the legal right of people to have a hearing before being imprisoned—a right known as *habeas corpus*—would be suspended. Truman rejected Hoover's proposal, and later that year the president vetoed, or refused to sign, the McCarran Act, a bill that would allow radicals to be detained without habeas corpus during a national emergency. Congress overrode Truman's veto and passed the McCarran Act, but Hoover's plan for mass jailings was not put into action.

Six years later, frustrated by what he saw as the failure of the Supreme Court, Congress, and the justice system to adequately protect the nation from subversion, Hoover set up the Counter Intelligence Program (COINTELPRO) within the Federal Bureau of Investigation. Through this program he directed FBI agents to investigate potentially dangerous organizations and movements—and not just to investigate them, but to infiltrate them, interfere with their operations, and disrupt them.

COINTELPRO's targets ranged from the Ku Klux Klan, a white-supremacy group, to the Black Panther Party, an African-American organization that included many political radicals. Also under COINTELPRO's eye were socialists, communists, antiwar groups, the women's rights movement, and religious and student organizations. Through COINTEL-PRO, the FBI maintained secret files on political figures such as President John F. Kennedy. The program paid particular attention to the growing civil rights movement. Agents put together thick files on individuals such as Martin Luther King Jr. and on groups such as the Congress for Racial Equality and the National Association for the Advancement of Colored People. "Dirty tricks" used by Federal Bureau of Investigation agents in the program included publishing and distributing false information about people and groups; harassing people with anonymous phone calls and anonymous or forged letters, including letters to their spouses to try to destroy their marriages; pressuring third parties such as landlords and school officials to make life difficult for the targets; unfairly singling out targets for tax audits, traffic tickets, and other harassment under the law; and even beatings and break-ins.

COINTELPRO's activities continued for fifteen years. In 1971 radicals in Pennsylvania got up to some dirty tricks of their own. They stole files from an FBI office and leaked them to the press. At first some newspapers hesitated to publish the material, but eventually the contents of the files—including information about COINTELPRO operations—became public. The criticism that followed these revelations led Hoover to declare that COINTELPRO was at an end.

Hoover died the following year, just before the news broke that the Republican president, Richard Nixon, had used advisers and staff members, some of whom had ties to the

FBI or the Central Intelligence Agency, to carry out secret operations against people and groups he viewed as enemies, including the Democratic Party. A bungled break-in at Democratic offices in the Watergate building in Washington, D.C., led eventually to jail sentences for some of the operatives and to an unscheduled change in the White House. Nixon resigned from office in 1974; Gerald Ford, his vice president, became president.

THE CHURCH REPORT

By the mid–1970s Congress and the public were asking just what was going on inside the FBI and the Central Intelligence Agency. The COINTELPRO and Watergate scandals, together with press reports suggesting that American intelligence agents had been involved in illegal operations overseas, made people call for a closer look at the operations of these agencies. Congress decided to investigate.

In 1975 Senator Frank Church, a Democrat from Idaho, was appointed to chair the Senate Select Subcommittee to Study Governmental Operations with Respect to Intelligence Activities—or, as most people called it, the Church Committee. The eleven-member committee, made up of Republican and Democratic senators, spent nine months interviewing eight hundred people and holding 271 hearings, 21 of which were public. The results were published in a series of fourteen volumes in 1975 and 1976. Together these volumes are known as the Church Report.

Some of the volumes bore alarming titles such as "Unauthorized Storage of Toxic Agents" and "Mail Opening." Others focused on the activities of the FBI and the Internal Revenue Service, the federal tax agency. Consisting of transcripts of hearings, reprints of documents and other exhibits, and the

Senator Frank Church (D-ID) was the author of a report that revealed the manifold abuses against civil liberties and privacy committed by the CIA in the name of protecting national security.

notes and reports of the committee members, the volumes made for unsettling reading—even though the Church Committee complained that the Central Intelligence Agency (CIA) refused to allow full, independent review of its files.

Part of the Church Report dealt with foreign matters, such as Central Intelligence Agency attempts to undermine or overthrow a democratically elected government in the South American nation of Chile. Other volumes dealt with domestic matters. These revealed the shocking extent to which Americans had been spied on by their own government. Between 1953 and 1973, for example, the Central Intelligence Agency had opened and photographed a quarter of a million private letters. During that same period FBI agents had created more than half a million files on individuals' political opinions and their activities, including activities that were protected by the First Amendment's guarantees of free speech and freedom of assembly.

Remembering

In 2001, when Congress was on the verge of making the Patriot Act law, Senator Patrick Leahy delivered a speech in which he spoke to his fellow senators about the era of COINTELPRO and the Church Report, two and a half decades earlier. He summed up one particularly disgraceful COINTELPRO operation carried out under Hoover's direction:

> The most notorious case was J. Edgar Hoover's vendetta against Dr. Martin Luther King Jr. The Church Committee documented the FBI's effort to discredit Dr. King by disclosing confidential information that was obtained from wiretaps and microphones targeted against him. The wiretaps were justified to the Kennedy and Johnson Administrations on the grounds that some of Dr. King's advisors were Communists, but this excuse allowed the FBI to mount continuous political surveillance to undermine Dr. King's effectiveness. The FBI disseminated allegedly derogatory information not only within the government, but to media and other private organizations including efforts to deny Dr. King the Nobel Peace Prize. Most vicious of all was the FBI's preparation of a composite tape recording that was sent to him anonymously with an apparent invitation to commit suicide.

"These methods of domestic political surveillance and covert manipulation and disruption have no place in a free society," Leahy went on to say. He reminded his listeners that Congress had passed the Foreign Surveillance Intelligence Act (FISA) in 1978 specifically to prevent the kind of abusive, unethical, and illegal activities that had been uncovered by the Church Committee.

The Patriot Act, Leahy said, was restoring some powers that

Past Mistakes

FBI director J. Edgar Hoover was so fanatical about rooting out real and imagined subversion that he and his agents broke the law to do so. Meanwhile, the Ku Klux Klan and other domestic terrorist groups roamed free.

FISA had taken away from law enforcement and intelligence agencies. This was a necessary step—it was vital that the United States do whatever it could to combat the new enemy, international terrorism. Yet Leahy hoped that it would not lead to a repetition of past problems.

"Much of the government's experience from the Cold War era before the mid–1970s warns us of the risks of abuse," he told the Senate as it prepared to vote on the Patriot Act. "Reasonable measures that we are taking to protect against international terrorism may have far-reaching ramifications beyond the immediate crisis. There has never been a greater need for Congressional vigilance to ensure against unnecessary and improper use of the wide discretion being granted by a new law."

"Too many people have been spied on by too many government agencies and too much information has been collected," said the Church Report. Congress agreed and passed a series of new laws designed to end the abuses by more strictly defining what agencies and agents could do, and by adding layers of oversight, or official supervision of agency activities. The most significant of these laws was the Foreign Intelligence Surveillance Act, or FISA. This law was the direct predecessor to the USA PATRIOT Act.

FISA

Congress passed the Foreign Intelligence Surveillance Act in 1978. The name of the act refers to its primary purpose: to govern the gathering of intelligence, or information, about agents acting inside the United States on behalf of a foreign power. The act focused on sabotage, espionage, terrorism, or conspiracy that was being planned or carried out on U.S. soil by foreign agents in the United States, or by Americans acting in the service of foreign powers.

FISA was a balancing act, just as the Patriot Act would be. Lawmakers tried to balance the need to safeguard the nation from foreign threats with the need to protect civil liberties, privacy, and other rights of citizens and legal residents of the United States. "The law recognized," writes free-speech historian Christopher M. Finan, "that the FBI needed the authority to conduct wiretapping and secret searches in pursuit of foreign agents engaged in spying in the United States. In the past, the FBI had simply assumed it had this authority."

After the Church Report, however, Congress was no longer willing to let the Federal Bureau of Investigation and the Central Intelligence Agency operate so freely that the rights of lawful citizens and residents could easily be violated. FISA created a mechanism for controlling and overseeing such operations. That mechanism was the Foreign Intelligence Surveillance Court, often referred to as the FISA court.

One of the FISA court's most important responsibilities was—and still is—granting the warrants that allow investigators to conduct search and surveillance operations. FISA brought about a significant change in the way such warrants are granted. Under ordinary circumstances, a law enforcement officer who is investigating a crime may want to search a suspect's home, read mail, or listen in on private conversations. To do so, the officer must first obtain a warrant issued by a court. To get the warrant, the officer must demonstrate "probable cause," which means there must be good reason for believing that evidence of a specific crime may be found. The officer or other law enforcement official, in other words, must tell the court what the investigators are looking for.

Under FISA, however, a federal agent who is investigating someone suspected of acting for a foreign power and who wants to use secret surveillance—such as wiretapping or searching without the knowledge of the suspect—would apply to the FISA court for a warrant. The 1978 act required that the request for a warrant had to show that the primary purpose of the investigation was to collect foreign intelligence, but the agent did not have to tie the request to a specific crime or a particular type of evidence. In this way, agents could gather evidence about suspected spies, saboteurs, or terrorists at an earlier stage in the investigation, without having to prove that a particular crime had been committed or was being planned.

FISA established that the court would consist of seven federal district court judges appointed by the Chief Justice of the Supreme Court to serve for terms of seven years. The operations of the court are veiled in secrecy, for the sake of security. Each year, however, the Department of Justice must present Congress with a report showing the number of requests for warrants made to the court, and the number granted. Although these reports reveal nothing about the suspects or the investigations, they do show that the FISA court grants the vast majority of requests. In 2007, for example, the court received 2,371 applications "to conduct electronic surveillance and physical search for foreign intelligence purposes only." It granted 2,370 of them.

BRINGING DOWN THE WALL

One of FISA's key purposes was to keep intelligence about foreign activities in the United States (or activities influenced by a foreign power) from mingling with information that was part of a criminal investigation. The provisions of the act, as well as regulations that were added later, prevented intelligence agents and criminal investigators from sharing information. One reason for this was to prevent foreign intelligence suspects from being unfairly harassed by law enforcement officers—someone who was being watched as a possible spy, for example, being repeatedly pulled over by traffic police.

Another reason for keeping intelligence gathering separate from criminal prosecution was to protect the criminal cases. This was necessary because intelligence agents operating under FISA followed different legal rules than crime investigators. Intelligence agents did not have to show "probable cause" before conducting a search or surveillance—in other words, they did not have to state that they were looking for evidence of a specific crime. Because crime investigators did not operate under FISA, however, they were still required to show probable cause for searching a suspect's home or listening in on private conversations. If a Central Intelligence Agency agent passed information to an FBI agent, and that information produced evidence that was used against an accused criminal in court, the case against the accused criminal might be thrown out of court because the evidence had been improperly acquired.

Over time, FISA created what former attorney general Ashcroft has described as a wall between government departments: barriers to the sharing of information among the military, the Central Intelligence Agency, federal prosecutors, and the FBI, or even between agents within the FBI if one of them was working on a criminal case and the other was gathering foreign intelligence. These barriers grew terribly frustrating to some law enforcement and intelligence agents who felt that the wall, originally intended to prevent abuses and improper evidence sharing, had grown too high. Now it was preventing investigators and agents from doing their best to protect the nation.

In August 2001 an FBI intelligence agent was investigating two known Al-Qaeda members in the United States. He wanted to track them, but the only way he could do so was through information in the hands of criminal investigators in the FBI. Legal experts within the FBI refused to allow the bureau's criminal investigators to become involved in the intelligence case, claiming that the wall of regulation prevented it. The frustrated agent wrote back to his superiors, saying, "Someday someone will die and, wall or not, the public will not understand why we were not more effective and throwing every resource we had at certain 'problems.'"Less than a month later, the two Al-Qaeda men took part in the 9/11 attack, flying a hijacked plane into the Pentagon.

Law enforcement officials have stated that they don't know whether, if the wall had not been in place, they would have been able to track the Al-Qaeda operatives, discover their plans, and prevent 9/11 from happening. Ashcroft has called it "a big maybe." After 9/11, however, he and others in the Department of Justice and in the White House were determined that the wall had to come down. Removing barriers and streamlining the sharing of information would be key features of the new Patriot Act.

MEANWHILE, IN THE LIBRARY . . .

After 1978, with COINTELPRO receding into history and FISA enacted, Americans might have thought that they were safe from covert, or secret, spying into their private affairs. Ten years after Congress passed FISA, though, Americans learned about one area in which their privacy was not safe. That area was their reading habits.

In 1986 FBI agents visited libraries at the University of Maryland in College Park and spoke with the library staff. The agents asked the librarians to observe the people who used the library and "report anyone with a foreign-sounding name or foreign-sounding accent" to the FBI.

Library director Herbert N. Foerstel was disturbed by the notion of the FBI spying on library patrons simply because they appeared foreign. He instructed the staff to keep all library records confidential, and he wrote about the incident in the state's library association newsletter. Foerstel also went on to research FBI surveillance of library patrons, using the Freedom of Information Act (FOIA), a law that requires the federal government to release all or part of certain documents and records upon request.

The following year Paula Kaufman, a director of libraries

Paula Kaufman, director of libraries at Columbia University, made the papers—and history—when she refused to participate in the Library Awareness Program, an FBI program in which librarians were asked to inform on what patrons read.

at New York City's Columbia University, wrote to the American Library Association to report that FBI agents had informed her of a Library Awareness Program in which agents recruited librarians "to report on who was reading what." Kaufman refused to participate, saying:

> The FBI's request to me to report on foreigners using our libraries is one with which I could not practically comply, even if our institution supported such cooperation, which it does not; even if such a request did not contravene [go against] my professional ethics, which it does; even if it did not infringe upon the First Amendment and privacy rights of all library patrons, which it does; and even if it does not violate the laws of the State of New York, which it does.

On September 18, 1987, the *New York Times* published Kaufman's letter. This was the first time the general public heard about library surveillance and the Library Awareness Program. Librarians and academics were already indignant about the program, and now others shared their indignation. Ridicule was part of the reaction, too. The *Washington Post*, for example, printed a cartoon showing an FBI agent skulking amid bookshelves in a library, spying on patrons, while a worried librarian telephoned to report "someone lurking around here who is acting kind of un-American."

Supporters of civil liberties and privacy rights felt that it was indeed un-American to keep track of people's reading. The Library Awareness Program was especially interested in learning who was reading scientific and technical materials, but the books, journals, and articles in question were not classified documents—they were freely available to students and other library users. Furthermore, the FBI had singled out foreigners for observation because it was concerned that Soviet intelligence agents might infiltrate libraries, but such profiling struck many as discriminatory.

Beyond those issues were the broader questions of whether library surveillance was truly useful, and whether people have the right to read what they want without worrying that their names will end up on a secret FBI list. Outrage over the Library Awareness Program reached new heights when a request for federal records under the Freedom of Information Act revealed that the FBI had investigated the librarians who had refused to cooperate with the program. It appeared that the bureau was questioning the loyalty of the librarians themselves. Many people saw in the Library Awareness Program ominous echoes of practices in past dictatorships and totalitarian states in which the government limited people's access to reading material. In Nazi Germany, for example, books by Jewish authors were removed from libraries and burned, while library patrons were encouraged to read volumes that praised the Nazi regime, and in Soviet Russia libraries were "purged" of works that appeared subversive to the ruling party and filled with works that supported it.

Congressional hearings into the Library Awareness Program revealed that the program had begun in the 1970s in New York City. It replaced an earlier program that was shut down after protests from the American Library Association and the National Education Association. In that earlier program, agents from a division of the Internal Revenue Service had pored over library records in search of people who were researching explosives. They had even gone so far as to investigate high school students who had written papers for their science classes.

Does reading about explosives mean that a library patron is a dangerous bomb maker, any more than reading about guns makes someone a murderer, or reading cookbooks makes someone a chef? The creators of the Library Awareness Program had felt that it simply made sense to look into libraries for evidence of people who might be researching ways to harm the nation and its citizens. Is preventing an attack a worthy reason to gather secret information about people's reading habits?

Those questions would arise again in the early twenty-first century. By the mid–1990s most states had passed new laws protecting the confidentiality of library records, and the FBI declared that it had ended its policy of recruiting librarians as general observers. Yet the bureau continued to claim the right to review the library records of specific suspects, and a few years later, when the Patriot Act went into force, libraries would again become battlegrounds in the conflict between national security and individual privacy.

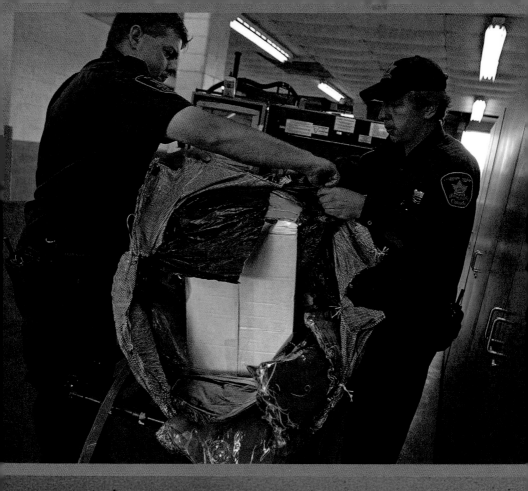

Canadian customs officers inspect a shipment of goods imported from the United States. Border patrol staff was greatly increased, and security tightened, as a result of the September 11, 2001, attacks.

CHAPTER SIX

Inside the Patriot Act

The USA PATRIOT Act became law in the fall of 2001. Immediately, law enforcement personnel, legal scholars, and civil rights activists across the land began sifting through the lengthy document, interpreting and debating the many provisions of the Act.

From the start, supporters of the Patriot Act claimed that it provided sufficient safeguards for civil rights and liberties while giving government the necessary tools to fight terrorism. Critics of the act, however, argued that it needlessly violated civil rights and liberties that are guaranteed under the U.S. Constitution. They charged that the Patriot Act was passed in haste, by a Congress that acted out of fear, not forethought. In their view, the act gave such broad powers to the executive branch of government—including the president, the Department of Justice, the Federal Bureau of Investigation, and the Central Intelligence Agency—that the rights of ordinary citizens were at risk.

In order to weigh the pros and cons of the Patriot Act, it

is necessary to know what the act contains. The full text of the act is available from a number of online sources, including the Department of Justice website. It contains numerous references to earlier laws—including the Electronic Communications Privacy Act, the Foreign Intelligence Surveillance Act, and the Money Laundering Control Act—that the Patriot Act amended or absorbed.

The Patriot Act begins with the heading "An Act To deter and punish terrorist acts in the United States and around the world, to enhance law enforcement investigatory tools, and for other purposes." Next is a table of contents that shows that the Patriot Act is divided into ten titles. Each title deals with a particular aspect of the act and contains a number of sections, which are basically individual laws. Some sections are more significant or controversial than others because they represent new or greatly expanded powers for the executive branch of government. Among them are sections that supporters of the act see as vital tools for protecting the country and its people, and that critics of the act regard as infringements of civil liberties.

PROTECTION FROM TERRORISM

Title I, "Enhancing Domestic Security Against Terrorism," contains sections 101 through 106 of the act. The first section established a fund within the Department of the Treasury to pay for expenses connected with the war on terror, including any rewards that the government might offer for information about suspected terrorists, or for their capture. The second section, referring to acts of violence against Arabs and Muslims that had taken place in the United States after 9/11, stated that only individuals, not ethnic, religious, or racial groups, could be held responsible for actions. This part of the Patriot Act condemned attacks on people because of their ethnic or religious identity. It called on the nation to treat Arab Americans, Muslim Americans, and South Asian Americans with justice and complete equality.

The next three sections increased Federal Bureau of Investigation funding; allowed the attorney general to call on the military for assistance in certain kinds of terrorism attacks; and instructed the Secret Service to set up a unit to deal with electronic crimes, such as terrorist attacks on communications networks or databases. The final section of Title I was intended to help the federal government follow terrorism's money trails and hit terrorists in the pocketbook. It expanded the executive branch's authority over financial transactions within the United States, and it also gave the president the power to seize money or other property that belonged to hostile foreigners in the United States.

SURVEILLANCE

Title II, "Enhanced Surveillance Procedures," contains sections 201 through 225. These sections of the Patriot Act revised FISA. They increased the government's power to carry out domestic surveillance against both citizens and noncitizens.

Various sections of Title II broadened the government's authority to intercept wire, oral, and electronic communications relating to terrorism and computer fraud; regulated the hiring of translators by the Federal Bureau of Investigation; enlarged the FISA court from seven to eleven judges; allowed voice mails to be seized with a warrant; allowed providers of wireless communication services to reveal information about their customers if they thought doing so would protect someone from physical harm; gave the Federal

Bureau of Investigation authority to examine businesses' records during terrorism investigations; and removed the right of privacy from computer trespassers (people using computers without permission).

Section 203 allowed investigators in various federal agencies to share all information related to foreign intelligence without a court order. Section 206 allowed the use of roving wiretaps, which meant that investigators would no longer have to get a warrant to tap each phone a suspect used. Instead, they could wiretap any phone used by the suspect. If suspects used multiple or disposable phones and changed them frequently, for example, agents would not have to get a new warrant each time, and the suspects could not count on having a few surveillance-free days while agents waited for the new warrant. Law enforcement and intelligence officials had wanted roving wiretaps for some time, so that they could move as quickly as the suspects they were investigating. The use of roving wiretaps, however, also meant that the agents might eavesdrop on the conversations of many innocent people, because they could monitor every phone used by a suspect, regardless of how many other people used that phone.

Section 213 of Title II lifted the requirement that suspects be notified of a search, and provided with copies of search warrants, at the time of the search. By authorizing a delay between the search and the notification, 213 permitted so-called sneak and peek warrants. Under this section investigators could secretly look for physical or electronic evidence without notifying suspects that they had been searched until "a reasonable period" afterward.

Section 214 dealt with two devices that investigators have long used in telephone surveillance: pen registers and trap-and-trace devices. Pen registers record the numbers dialed for outgoing calls, while trap-and-trace devices record the numbers of incoming calls. Neither device captures the content of the calls, only the numbers dialed. Under FISA, an investigator did not have to show probable cause that using one of these devices would produce evidence in a specific crime—all that was needed was to claim that the search was relevant, or related, to an investigation concerning foreign intelligence.

Under Section 214 of the Patriot Act, the FISA rule of relevance was broadened to apply to criminal as well as intelligence investigations. Section 216 of the act applied the rule to the Internet, allowing investigators to obtain records of a suspect's computer use, including e-mail addresses. Section 220 stated that a search warrant for electronic evidence— such as a suspect's Internet use—is valid anywhere in the country, not just in the jurisdiction where it was issued, as was the case with traditional warrants. The act's supporters pointed out that these changes were necessary to keep pace with technology. In a world of instant worldwide and nationwide communication by computer and cell phone, agents could not effectively fight terrorism and crime if they were forced to follow rules that dated from the era of written mail and telephones that were anchored to a single location.

Section 215 of Title II allowed investigators to get warrants to examine tangible—that is, physical—objects without showing probable cause of an illegal act. Under this provision, an investigator can, for example, examine records of a suspect's activities that are possessed by third parties, such as stores, libraries, and banks. To obtain the warrant, the investigator must state only that it is needed to gather foreign intelligence or to protect against terrorism.

The final sections of Title II covered various topics. One

dealt with trade barriers against nations or groups linked with terrorism. Another provided that communications companies, landlords, employers, and others who help the Federal Bureau of Investigation during investigations can be paid for their costs. Still other sections outlined the penalties for agents who disclose confidential information without authority; allowed people to sue the United States for violations of the act; and established a "sunset" for certain sections of the title, meaning that these sections would expire at the end of 2005 unless renewed by Congress. Section 225 granted immunity (freedom from lawsuits or penalties) to telecommunications companies, landlords, employers, and others who disclose information or otherwise help the Federal Bureau of Investigation in its investigations.

MONEY MATTERS

Title III is both part of the Patriot Act and a separate act of its own, called the International Money Laundering Abatement and Anti-Terrorist Financing Act of 2001. Most of this act's seventy-seven sections are amendments to two previous laws, the Bank Secrecy Act of 1970 and the Money Laundering Control Act of 1986.

Money laundering is the process of "cleaning" money gained through illegal activities, or from illegal or prohibited sources, by passing it through legitimate businesses, banks, or financial transactions to make it seem that the money was earned legally. Typically money laundering involves three steps: placing the money in a financial institution such as a bank; layering it, or sending it through as many steps as possible to change its form; and then reintroducing it to the economy in the form of legitimate funds. Possible changes during the layering step include moving the money to many other bank accounts in multiple transfers, changing it into foreign currencies, passing it through foreign bank accounts, and buying expensive items such as gems or yachts that can be resold. The final step may involve investing the funds in a completely legitimate business, such as a restaurant or trucking company, that is owned by the money launderer or an associate. Money that has been laundered in this way is hard to trace to its "dirty" origins.

The Patriot Act made it harder for both criminals and terrorists to launder money by tightening some of the rules governing banks and financial institutions, especially those that do business internationally. Banks were placed under increased responsibility to report suspicious transactions, for example. Title III of the Patriot Act also stiffened the penalties for smuggling money and counterfeiting it.

ON THE BORDER

After 9/11, investigators discovered that some of the hijackers had entered the United States on student visas, which had expired. These individuals had violated immigration law by remaining in the country after their visas had expired, but the Immigration and Naturalization Service had not tracked their whereabouts or their status. This news made many people feel that the nation's immigration system had broken down. It had failed to keep dangerous aliens (foreign-born noncitizens) out of the country, and it had failed to keep tabs on those who had been allowed in. Title IV of the Patriot Act, "Protecting the Border," was meant to correct those problems.

The title consists of twenty-eight sections designed to make it harder for terrorists or suspected terrorists to enter the United States, and easier for the Immigration and Naturalization Service and the Justice Department to track visitors or immigrants once they enter the country. One section of this title tripled the Border Patrol staff along the U.S. border with Canada, which lawmakers perceived as having been neglected in comparison with efforts made to strengthen border security with Mexico. Others called for the use of technological tools such as passport-reading machines and automated fingerprint readers at the nation's entry points, and authorized an increase in the monitoring of student visas.

Section 411 defined the ways people can be refused permission to enter the United States on grounds of association with terrorism. Someone known to belong to a terrorist organization will be denied entry, of course. So will someone who has voiced public support or encouragement for terrorists, or who belongs to any group that, in the opinion of the U.S. secretary of state, "undermines United States efforts to reduce or eliminate terrorism." Someone who has associated with a terrorist may be refused permission to enter, even if the person did not know that the terrorist *was* a terrorist.

Section 412 gave Department of Justice officials the authority to detain, or jail, aliens who were suspected of being terrorists without charging them with crimes and without review by a judge. Under this provision, the attorney general can order someone to be held for up to seven days without demonstrating that the person poses a danger. Detention for longer periods, or indefinitely, is possible "if the release of the alien will threaten the national security of the United States or the safety of the community or any person."

REMOVING OBSTACLES

The eight sections of Title V, "Removing Obstacles to Investigating Terrorism," are concerned with ways of investigating, capturing, and prosecuting terrorists. The first four sections authorized the attorney general and the secretary of state to pay rewards for information used to capture terrorists; ordered DNA samples to be collected from convicted terrorists and violent criminals; and allowed intelligence investigators to share the information they obtained through electronic surveillance or physical searches with other federal law enforcement agencies in order to prevent terrorist attacks, sabotage, or espionage. These provisions were steps toward removing the barriers against information sharing that had developed under FISA.

Section 505 of Title V deals with powers called national security authorities. FISA had given the director and deputy directors of the Federal Bureau of Investigation the power to write documents called national security letters. When presented with one of these documents, a bank, credit card company, Internet service provider, or credit bureau must give the FBI access to customer records and may not inform the customer that his or her records have been examined. A national security letter, unlike a warrant, does not have to be approved or reviewed by a judge or by any authority outside the Federal Bureau of Investigation. Before the Patriot Act, only senior officials in the Bureau could issue national security letters. Section 505 of the act gave that power to FBI field offices.

The next section of Title V allowed the Secret Service, which is charged with protecting the president and vice president and their families, to take part in investigations of computer crimes. The final two sections authorized the Federal Bureau of Investigation to look at confidential educational records and surveys if those records were believed to be related to a terrorism investigation.

FOR THE VICTIMS

Title VI of the Patriot Act, "Providing for Victims of Terrorism, Public Safety Officers, and Their Families," concerned payments to people who are injured in terrorist attacks, or to the families of people who are killed. This part of the act governs the money paid by the government to public safety workers, such as police and fire officers. It also regulates the funds that are set up to manage charitable donations to other victims, such as the outpouring of millions of dollars in aid that Americans gave to victims of the 9/11 attacks.

WORKING TOGETHER

Title VII, "Increased Information Sharing for Critical Infrastructure Protection," has just one section. It amended an earlier law called the Omnibus Crime Control and Safe Streets Act of 1968, which had allowed the Federal Bureau of Investigation to help state and local law enforcement agencies, and also nonprofit organizations, to fight criminal activities that cross the borders of state and local jurisdictions. The Patriot Act added terrorism and terrorist conspiracies to the types of criminal activities affected by the earlier act. It also set aside funds to establish a communications and information-sharing system, involving both new software and new procedures, that would enable Federal Bureau of Investigation, state, and local authorities to work together effectively in the event of a terrorist attack.

DEFINING TERRORISM

Title VIII, "Strengthening the Criminal Laws Against Terrorism," contains seventeen sections. Some of them defined terrorism by listing and describing various types of activity. Others specified the penalties to be dealt out to those who commit terrorist crimes.

Section 808 defined the federal crime of terrorism. The lengthy list of actions includes: using weapons of mass destruction; arson or bombing of government-owned property that could result in someone's death; torture; hijacking; kidnapping, or assassination of political figures; attacks on American tourists abroad; violence at airports.

Section 802 introduced a new category of crime called domestic terrorism. It includes activities that are dangerous to human life and that violate U.S. criminal laws. Such criminal activity is considered to be terrorism if it appears to be intended to frighten or influence the American people, to influence government policy, or to affect government operations. This definition of domestic terrorism is broad enough to include crimes committed by, for example, environmental activists or abortion protestors.

Other sections of Title VIII outlined punishments for attacking mass transportation; for using biological weapons; for committing computer crimes, or cybercrimes, such as fraud or hacking into a protected database; and for helping terrorists, either by sheltering them or giving them money or expert advice. To increase the nation's protection from computer crimes, and to make it easier for such crimes to be prosecuted, Title VIII also authorized the attorney general to set up computer forensics labs in different regions of the country, and to increase support to existing labs. Section 816 granted $50 million a year for those purposes.

GATHERING INTELLIGENCE

The eight sections of Title IX, "Improved Intelligence," are concerned with the sharing of information between the Central Intelligence Agency, Federal Bureau of Investigation, and other agencies such as the Department of Energy and the State Department. Title IX updated earlier laws governing communication between federal agencies. For example, it required the director of the Central Intelligence Agency to share foreign intelligence about terrorism with the Federal Bureau of Investigation. In turn, the Federal Bureau of Investigation was instructed to pass on to the Central Intelligence Agency any information related to foreign intelligence that it acquired during a criminal investigation. Title IX further demolished the information-sharing barrier by not just allowing but requiring agencies to share information about terrorism and foreign intelligence.

Since 2004 the interagency communications authorized by the Patriot Act have been coordinated by the director of National Intelligence. The office of director of National Intelligence was created in that year by the Intelligence Reform and Terrorism Prevention Act. The director is the formal head of the nation's intelligence community, which includes the Central Intelligence Agency, the Department of Homeland Security, the military, the Federal Bureau of Investigation, the Drug Enforcement Administration, and more.

Title IX also provided for the creation of a National Virtual Translation Center, a resource for investigators dealing with written and spoken communications in various languages; for the creation of a center for tracking foreign assets; and for government officials to be trained in how to recognize and use foreign intelligence.

EVERYTHING ELSE

The tenth and final title of the Patriot Act is headed "Miscellaneous." It contains sixteen sections covering matters not included in the previous titles. Section 1001, for example, directed the Department of Justice to assign one official to review claims about violations of civil rights and civil liberties under the Patriot Act, and to report to Congress on those claims twice a year. Other sections provided funds for drug enforcement training in Asia; for antiterrorism training to be given to police and emergency medical technicians in the United States; and for the Federal Bureau of Investigation to use in putting together a list of suspected terrorists' names and sharing that list with airlines. This part of the Patriot Act also authorized the U.S. military to hire private contractors to provide security services—essentially, mercenaries—as it has done during the war in Iraq.

President George W. Bush signed the USA PATRIOT Act into law on October 26, 2001, a month and a half after the terrorist attacks of 9/11. He declared, "The bill before me takes account of the new realities and dangers posed by modern terrorists. It will help law enforcement to identify, to dismantle, to disrupt, and to punish terrorists before they strike."

As the Patriot Act went into effect, Americans hoped that the president was right, and that the act would protect the United States from attack while slowing the spread of terrorist activity around the world. Some Americans also wondered what other effects the Patriot Act would have on civil liberties, privacy, and law enforcement. Out of their concerns would rise questions about the Patriot Act, as well as challenges to it.

Barry Reingold, a sixty-year-old from California, was questioned by FBI agents because he was overheard expressing criticism of the bombings in Afghanistan, and of President Bush.

CHAPTER SEVEN

Controversy and Reauthorization

Even before the Patriot Act became law it was under fire from critics—inside Congress and outside it—who felt that the act bent or even broke the Constitution. Librarians defied the act, cities and towns proclaimed their opposition to it, and bumper stickers asked, "How would a patriot act?"

Organizations such as the American Civil Liberties Union (ACLU) struggled to call attention to what they saw as serious flaws in the Patriot Act, chiefly threats to privacy and civil liberties. On the other side of the issue, supporters of the act strove to convince Congress and the public that the law was necessary, effective, and harmless to civil liberties.

The debate over the Patriot Act gained heat as the four-year "sunset" deadline approached, with some of the act's most controversial sections scheduled to expire. The question of whether to reauthorize, or renew, those sections became a congressional battle. Other clashes took place in libraries, town halls, and courtrooms across the country and on thousands of blogs and websites, as people and groups argued passionately about whether the Patriot Act was saving America or shredding the Bill of Rights.

CRITICIZING THE PATRIOT ACT

Opinions about the Patriot Act generally followed a political pattern. Critics of the act tended to come from the part of the American political spectrum that is called the left. They were liberal and often belonged to the Democratic Party. Supporters of the act tended to come from the right, meaning that they were conservative and usually associated with the Republican Party. Yet there have also been liberals among supporters of the Patriot Act and conservatives among its critics.

Criticism of the Patriot Act was fueled by incidents that took place across the United States in the wake of 9/11. In October 2001, for example, a sixty-year-old San Francisco, California, man named Barry Reingold entered into a heated political debate at his local gym. By that time the United States had started dropping bombs on Afghanistan, and Reingold was critical both of the bombings and of President Bush. A week later, two Federal Bureau of Investigation agents came to Reingold's apartment and questioned him about his political beliefs.

The following summer, security officers at San Francisco International Airport detained two women who were there to take a flight to Boston. Jan Adams and Rebecca Gordon, who were traveling for a family visit, submitted to hours of questioning by officials before they were allowed to leave the airport. The two women's names had apparently shown up on a secret government "no-fly" list of people who were considered too dangerous to allow on aircraft. Adams and Gordon were not told why their names were on the list, or what they could do to have their names removed from it. The two women's names could have been added to the no-fly list by mistake—many such mistakes were revealed in the media during months and years after 9/11. Or the government may have labeled Adams and Gordon "dangerous" because they were peace activists who were known to hold antiwar beliefs.

The case of Andrew O'Connor, an attorney who worked as a public defender, unfolded in early 2003 in New Mexico. O'Connor was using a computer at a library in Santa Fe to surf the Internet when four police officers surrounded him. Secret Service agents then handcuffed, detained, and questioned O'Connor. His crime? During a political discussion, O'Connor, who disagreed with the president's position on various issues, had used the phrase "Bush is out of control." Someone had reported the remark to authorities, who treated O'Connor as a threat to the president.

These and many similar incidents reported in the nation's news media, which seemed like clear threats to the right to free speech guaranteed by the First Amendment to the Constitution, led civil libertarians to conclude that the U.S. government was abusing its power. Some criticism of the Patriot Act was linked to a more general disapproval of the Bush administration's policies. Civil libertarians, in particular, had been wary of the Bush administration even before 9/11 and the Patriot Act. They tended to view the Patriot Act as part of a larger Bush administration attack on civil liberties.

Attorney and professor Elaine Cassel, for example, made her position crystal-clear in the title of her 2004 book, *The War on Civil Liberties: How Bush and Ashcroft Have Dismantled the Bill of Rights.* Cassel focused on "the Bush administration's curtailment of civil liberties and how this policy is directly tied to the war on terrorism. Like the war on terrorism, this war was undertaken in the name of national security and in defense of 'freedom.'" In Cassel's opinion, "the rule of law and the Constitution" became victims of the Bush administration's war on civil liberties. To those who shared this view, the executive branch of the federal government seemed to be using the Patriot Act as a shield behind which to strip away people's civil rights and liberties. They argued that the security gained by such actions was, at best, uncertain.

CONTROVERSIAL ISSUES

Criticism of the Patriot Act, for the most part, has focused on certain sections that disturb civil libertarians and experts in constitutional law. These sections concern information sharing; invasion of privacy; the detention and deportation of people thought to have ties to terrorism; the treatment of enemy combatants, including torture; and a principle known as ideological exclusion.

Information Sharing

With the passage of the Foreign Intelligence Surveillance Act (FISA) in 1978, Congress had built a "wall" to prevent the sharing of information among various law enforcement and intelligence agencies. Other laws and policies strengthened that wall—and with good reason. Revelations that the FBI had secretly amassed intelligence files on Martin Luther King Jr. and thousands of other law-abiding U.S. citizens had driven home the danger of allowing the unlimited and unnecessary sharing of information.

After 9/11, however, the Justice Department argued that the wall had gotten too high and too strong. Without barriers to timely information sharing, for example, two of the 9/11 hijackers, Nawaf al-Hazmi and Khalid al-Mihdhar, might have been under surveillance, or in custody, before the attack. The

Central Intelligence Agency had believed that these two suspected terrorists were in the United States, but the Federal
Bureau of Investigation did not learn about their possible
presence in the country until August 2001, shortly before
the attack. Something similar happened in the case of Zacarias Moussaoui, who was not one of the hijackers but who
later pleaded guilty to being part of the conspiracy. Before
9/11 Moussaoui was known to both the Central Intelligence
Agency and the FBI, but the two agencies had not shared
information about him or coordinated their investigations.

The Patriot Act broke down the wall with Sections 203(b)
and 203(d), which not only allowed but required the sharing
of information among agencies in cases of suspected terrorism. Yet critics of the Patriot Act argued that those provisions
were not necessary—that, in fact, the wall was not as big a
barrier to interagency communication as the Justice Department claimed. Official channels for sharing certain kinds of
information existed before the Patriot Act; information submitted to a grand jury, for example, could always be shared.
Agents often failed to use these channels, however, perhaps
because of poor training or fear of making a mistake.

Section 218 of the Patriot Act also had to do with the
"wall." This provision lowered the standard for wiretaps and
searches in cases where intelligence agents were investigating suspected agents of foreign powers. Before the Patriot
Act, investigators had to claim that the intelligence investigation was the "primary purpose" of the wiretap or search.
Under Section 218, they had only to say that it was a "significant purpose." This made it easier for investigators to carry
out wiretaps or searches in cases that were only indirectly
related to terrorism, or unrelated to it. Critics of the act feared
that under this rule, an investigation supposedly against

terrorism might turn into a criminal investigation—but one that could be carried out in secret under the Patriot Act. In other words, it could be used against anyone the authorities had reason to suspect of any form of wrongdoing, effectively cutting the court system out of the process. Writing for the American Bar Association's *Human Rights Magazine* soon after the passage of the Patriot Act, lawyer and professor John Podesta called for careful monitoring of how Section 218 was used: "Section 218 is an important tool for counterterrorism but, since probable cause is not required under FISA, it also raises the possibility that U.S. citizens who are not terrorists could have their homes searched and communications monitored without probable cause. Therefore, section 218 deserves special attention when it expires in four years."

For many critics, the biggest problem was not that the Patriot Act tore down the wall that blocked information sharing between agencies. The problem was that the act went too far and was not sufficiently specific. The act allowed agents to request or share information without explaining why the information was necessary. Critics argued that agents or agencies that shared information should be required to say why they had to do so, and that the information that could be shared should be limited to things directly related to espionage and terrorism. Without such safeguards, the power granted by the act could be misused. For example, if the FBI were wiretapping a peace activist and turned up evidence of drug use, and then turned that information over to the police, that would overstep the intended provisions of the act.

Invasion of Privacy
The Patriot Act contained many areas of concern to privacy advocates. One was the "roving wiretap," which let

investigators get a single permit to tap all of the communication devices that a suspect used, rather than getting a separate permission for each device. While this provision of the Patriot Act made investigators' jobs easier, it also made it easier for them to overhear nonsuspects who shared or used the same devices. This, said privacy advocates, increased the likelihood of "fishing" for possible evidence of wrongdoing by people who were never identified as targets of an investigation. And this brought up bad memories of the witch hunts of the 1950s Red Scare, when those suspected of being communists or homosexuals or, seemingly, anything else the FBI's   J. Edgar Hoover didn't like, were harassed and sometimes had their livelihoods destroyed.

"Sneak and peek" warrants also set off alarm bells. Formally known as delayed notification warrants, these documents let investigators search a suspect's home without notifying the suspect that a search has taken place. The language of the Patriot Act, said critics, was unnecessarily broad. Rather than limiting sneak and peek searches to cases with a clear link to terrorism or espionage, the law let FBI agents perform such searches on criminals such as drug dealers. This represented a dramatic loosening of the rules that formerly applied to criminal investigations—rules that had been established on the basis of constitutionally protected civil rights.

The American Civil Liberties Union claimed at one point that "88 percent of these search warrants, which can still be kept secret for months or years, have been obtained by the Bush administration in cases that have nothing to do with terrorism." On the other side of this issue, Deputy Attorney General James B. Comey has pointed out that the delayed notification search warrant has been used as a tool in law enforcement since the 1970s and that "the Supreme Court concluded in

1979 that it was reasonable under the Fourth Amendment to use this tool." Before the Patriot Act, criminal investigators had to request delayed notification warrants on a case-by-case basis to judges who evaluated the need for them. The act created a specific statute, or law, eliminating any doubt that the warrants would be made available when requested.

Section 215 of the Patriot Act also received strong criticism. This provision allowed investigators to seize "tangible" or physical objects such as receipts, records, and other documents from third parties such as bookstores, libraries, banks, and more. The only requirement for such seizures was that they be carried out "in connection with" a terrorism investigation—a term that privacy advocates said was so vague as to be meaningless. Privacy advocates argued that investigators should be required to provide more specific grounds for requesting private records. They also claimed that Section 215's "gag rule," which said that a person who is required to turn over someone else's records could not mention it to the suspect or anyone else, should be lifted because it violated free speech rights.

Detention and Deportation
Violating or even threatening the liberty and privacy of U.S. citizens is bad, many would agree. But what about the rights of noncitizens? Sections 411 and 412 of the Patriot Act strengthened the government's authority to take action against aliens, or people who are not citizens of the United States—whether they are inside the United States legally or illegally. The Patriot Act's strictest provisions are aimed at aliens. According to David D. Cole, a constitutional scholar and author of *Enemy Aliens: Double Standards and Constitutional Freedoms in the War on Terrorism*, a double standard

"allows American citizens to declare that they will accept any sacrifice of liberty that supports the war on terrorism, so long as that sacrifice is borne by noncitizens."

The Patriot Act defined "terrorism" more broadly for non-citizens than for citizens, for example. In the case of aliens, support for any organization that has ever used violence—even when that support is for lawful activities—could be defined as "terrorist activity." Any threat to use a weapon for anything other than direct personal gain would also fit the definition. An alien suspected of terrorist activity, or even of having associated with people who were suspected of terrorist activity, could be taken into custody and detained without formal charges indefinitely.

In the wake of 9/11, many Muslim and Middle Eastern immigrants who later proved to have no connection whatsoever to terrorism were detained in this way, sometimes for months. In a 2003 letter to FBI director Robert Mueller, Federal Bureau of Investigation special agent Coleen Rowley wrote, "The vast majority of the one thousand plus persons 'detained' in the wake of 9-11 did not turn out to be terrorists."

The unjust penalties inflicted on some immigrants went far beyond detention, as the case of Maher Arar shows. Born in Syria, Arar became a citizen of Canada. In 2002, while he was returning to his home in Ottawa from a family vacation in Tunisia, he had a stopover at a New York airport. There immigration officials seized him, questioned him for eight hours, and then sent him to solitary confinement in a detention center. All he was told was that he had been seen with terrorism suspects in Ottawa. When Arar asked for a lawyer, he was told, "You are not an American citizen, you don't have a right to a lawyer."

The United States decided to deport Arar, but instead of returning him to Canada, where he held citizenship, American officials sent him to Syria, where he was imprisoned and tortured. It later turned out that Canadian intelligence officers had given inaccurate information about Arar to U.S. intelligence, but U.S. officials had not consulted with Canada before deporting him to Syria. It took the Canadian government a year of diplomatic efforts to win Arar's release. The Canadian government investigated Arar's claims of torture, found them to be true, and issued a public apology. Department of Justice officials in the United States, in contrast, refused to cooperate with the Canadian investigation and continued to say that the case had been properly handled.

Maher Arar is not the only individual who has been spirited away by U.S. officials, only to be mistreated in a secret location in a foreign country. Because counterterrorism operations under the Patriot Act are shrouded in secrecy, no one knows for certain how many such "renditions," to use the term favored by the Justice Department and the U.S. military, have taken place. Their number is certainly much smaller than the number of immigrants who have been detained within the United States on suspicion of terrorist activity and then deported because authorities uncovered a criminal charge or a violation of immigration law—in many cases, a violation that would not have resulted in deportation before 9/11. The Patriot Act has been used to enforce existing immigration laws more strictly than was previously the case.

Unlawful Combatants

Enemy combatants in the war on terror have been defined as belonging to a special legal category. The United States government and military have long used the term *enemy combatant* to refer to any individual involved in an armed conflict who could rightly be captured and imprisoned according to the rules of war—chiefly the international agreement called the Geneva Conventions. That agreement, among other things, governs the treatment of prisoners of war. Under the Geneva Conventions, a captured combatant must either be given the rights owed to a prisoner of war or prosecuted as a civilian, with the legal rights of any other defendant. Most often, an enemy combatant was a soldier in the armed forces of a state with which the United States was at war, but the term also applied to participants in civil wars and rebellions.

As the general counsel of the U.S. Defense Department pointed out in a 2002 memo for the Council on Foreign Relations, American law has recognized two categories of enemy combatants since the Geneva Conventions were ratified in the 1940s: lawful and unlawful. "Lawful combatants receive prisoner of war (POW) status and the protections of the Third Geneva Convention," wrote counsel William Haynes. "Unlawful combatants do not receive POW status and do not receive the full protections of the Third Geneva Convention."

The United States has conducted its treatment of the enemy combatants not under the Patriot Act but under two other authorities: a congressional resolution called "The Authorization for the Use of Military Force Against Terrorists," passed a week after 9/11, and a presidential military order, "Detention, Treatment, and Trial of Certain Non-Citizens in the War Against Terrorism," signed by President Bush under the War Powers Act in November 2001. Military and human-rights questions about the detainees at Guantanamo Bay, however, are often included in discussions of the Patriot Act because the treatment of people captured abroad is part of how the United States conducts its war on terror.

So, when U.S. forces went to war in Afghanistan after 9/11, they fought and captured members of militia and guerrilla groups, people who were technically civilians. The Bush administration determined that these prisoners were unlawful combatants because they belonged to terrorist groups that are not aligned with, or part of, a particular nation or state. Such prisoners captured abroad during wartime have been allowed to be detained under presidential authority, without specific charges and for indefinite lengths of time.

The detainees captured in the war on terror were held in a U.S. military prison at Guantanamo Bay in Cuba—a site often called Gitmo. There they have been investigated by the military and the Justice Department. If they were cleared of criminal charges, they were released to return to their homelands or to other nations—including Italy, the United Kingdom, Chad, Bermuda, and Saudi Arabia—that have agreed to accept them. By June 2009, more than five hundred such detainees had been released. Earlier that year President Barack Obama had announced a plan to close the Gitmo detention facility by 2010. Under this plan, the remaining detainees would be either cleared and released or transferred to military or federal prisons in the United States.

Trouble with Torture

After evidence came to light that some detainees held by the United States in Iraq and at Guantanamo Bay had received inhumane or abusive treatment, Americans found themselves debating the use of torture against enemy combatants. One question was whether the prisoners who had undergone "enhanced interrogation," as the Central Intelligence Agency called it, had been tortured or just harshly treated. A second question asked whether torture is a reliable method of

The use of torture at Guantanamo Bay led to a heated debate over whether those arrested as possible terrorists have fewer rights to humane treatment than others.

getting useful information. And a third question focused on whether the United States could or should torture prisoners —an act it has condemned when other countries do it— under any circumstances.

Early in the war on terror the Justice Department had prepared memos to justify the enhanced interrogation techniques. According to the Justice Department, these techniques did not amount to torture. When details began reaching the public in 2003 and 2004, however, most legal experts and members of the government agreed that at least one technique used against some detainees qualified as torture. That technique is an ancient practice known as waterboarding, in which a prisoner is forced to lie at an angle, with the feet higher than the head and the face covered by a cloth or hood. The interrogators then pour water continuously over the prisoner's nose and mouth, which creates the sensation of drowning. Justice Department memos that were released to the public in April 2009 revealed that one detainee with known ties to Al-Qaeda, Khalid Sheikh Mohammed, was waterboarded 183 times in the month of March 2003 alone. Another known Al-Qaeda operative, Abu Zubaydah, had been waterboarded 82 times in August 2002.

In 2005 Congress passed the Detainee Treatment Act, which states that detainees held by the United States will not be tortured. In January 2009, soon after taking office, President Barack Obama specifically banned the practice of waterboarding by U.S. agencies and armed forces, calling it torture. Obama also announced that no charges would be brought against the Central Intelligence Agency operatives who had waterboarded prisoners or the Bush administration officials who had authorized the acts.

One of the Bush administration officials, former vice president Dick Cheney, claimed that waterboarding had been a "success" and had produced information about terrorist plots. Michael Hayden, head of the Central Intelligence Agency under President Bush, also said, "The facts of the case are that the use of these techniques against these terrorists made us safer—it really did work." Other senior members of the intelligence community, however, denied that useful information had been gained through waterboarding.

On the broader question of whether torture produces useful information, opinions are divided. Psychological studies have shown that some people resist even harsh interrogation effectively; others find it hard to resist even mild interrogation. According to Darius Rejali, author of a 2007 history called *Torture and Democracy*, the problem is not that people who know things lie about them under torture—the problem is that people who don't know anything valuable say all kinds of things simply to gain relief from torture. As a result, "the torture of the ignorant and innocent overwhelms investigators with misleading information." Interrogators have no way of telling which of many statements made under torture are true, if any are. They must waste time investigating the false statements.

To many people, the question of whether torture works is beside the point. They feel that America should not use torture, because to do so lowers the nation to a barbaric level and violates its values. Others feel that in order to protect itself, America must do whatever is necessary and need not show greater concern for enemy combatants and detainees than terrorists have shown for Americans. Ethical debates about whether, or when, it is right to torture others are likely to continue long after the banning of waterboarding.

Ideological Exclusion
The Patriot Act was bad news for some aliens who were already in the United States. Section 411 also created problems for some who wanted to enter, either as immigrants or simply as temporary visitors. This provision allows the government to refuse entry into the country to anyone who "endorses or espouses terrorist activity or persuades others to endorse or espouse terrorist activity or support a terrorist organization." This wording is broad enough to include a great variety of spoken or written ideas, but the U.S. State Department encouraged officials to expand the wording to include "irresponsible expressions of opinion"—a phrase that could mean any ideas of which the State Department disapproved.

The practice of using the law to keep out unwelcome ideas, or to exclude people based on their words rather than their actions, is called ideological exclusion. It did not originate with the Patriot Act. For years, the U.S. government has used various laws—such as a 1952 immigration law called the McCarran-Walter Act—to keep people it considered "undesirable" from entering the country. Such undesirables included communists, socialists, political activists of all kinds, and writers and artists whose ideas the government did not like.

In 1990 a revised immigration law made it more difficult for the government to use ideological exclusion as a reason for keeping someone out of the United States, or for deporting someone who was already in the country. James R. Edwards Jr. is a historian of immigration policies who considers that excluding people who hold radical or extreme ideas from the country is a reasonable and necessary precaution. In his view, the 1990 changes "gutted ideological exclusion" and "loosened the legal and procedural barriers to entry by aliens who radically oppose the United States." Section 411 of the Patriot Act restored those barriers by giving officials a renewed, stronger legal basis for ideological exclusions.

Among the people who were denied permission to enter the United States on grounds of ideological exclusion in the decades before the Patriot Act were Nobel Prize–winning Colombian writer Gabriel García Márquez; Nobel Prize–winning Chilean poet Pablo Neruda; and John Lennon of the Beatles, who criticized U.S. actions during the Vietnam War in the 1970s. South African activist, Nobel Peace Prize–winner (1993), and president, Nelson Mandela, who until 2003 remained on a list of "undesirable aliens," had to obtain special permission to enter the United States. More recently, British hip-hop artist M.I.A. was prevented from entering the country in 2006 because some of her song lyrics had political elements. Tariq Ramadan, a Swiss Islamic scholar, had to resign a teaching position at the University of Notre Dame in

Indiana because the State Department withdrew his visa—even though the U.S. government later withdrew its claim that Ramadan had endorsed terrorist organizations by giving money to Islamic charities.

When Barack Obama, a Democrat, was elected to the presidency in 2008, civil libertarians and free-speech advocates hoped that he would reverse the Bush administration's policies of ideological exclusion. The new president had a chance to do so in early 2009, when the withdrawal of Tariq Ramadan's visa was challenged in federal appeals court. An assistant U.S. attorney representing the Obama administration, however, called upon the court not to overturn the earlier decision. The administration's position was that visa decisions are the business of the State Department, not the courts.

Free-speech advocates were disappointed by the Obama administration's decision not to intervene in the Ramadan case. Yet in a paper prepared for the Center for Immigration Studies, Edwards argues that although the First Amendment to the Constitution gives Americans the right to free speech, "The First Amendment does not guarantee absolute free speech. It does not protect treasonous speech by U.S. citizens; it should not be regarded as protecting seditious speech by aliens." In Edwards's view, it is common sense to prevent noncitizens whose spoken or written ideas "can reasonably be expected to incite dangerous, perhaps seditious, activities" against the United States from entering the country and spreading their beliefs. The National Coalition Against Censorship, however, is one of a number of groups that have voiced the opposing view: "The suggestion that the Executive Branch can exclude visitors who risk 'irresponsible expressions of opinion' should be a cause for alarm, shame, and defense of First Amendment rights."

Ideological exclusion continues to raise important questions for a nation that has enshrined freedom of speech as one of its most cherished values: How far should the government go in limiting its citizens' ability to hear other people's views? Is ideological exclusion a reasonable way to prevent real, harmful acts of terrorism, or is it simply a war on ideas?

TAKING A STAND

The Patriot Act sparked grassroots opposition. A number of student organizations, religious groups, labor unions, and other associations passed resolutions condemning or criticizing the parts of the Patriot Act that they interpreted as threats to civil liberties, or calling for stronger protection for those liberties. Many communities enacted similar measures.

According to the Bill of Rights Defense Committee, between January 2002 and December 2007, "resolutions and ordinances critical of the USA PATRIOT Act and other laws and policies that diminish civil liberties" were passed by 406 county or local governments and by the legislatures of eight states: Alaska, California, Colorado, Hawaii, Idaho, Maine, Montana, and Vermont. These resolutions had no legal force against the Patriot Act, which is a federal statute. They served as public statements of values, however, and as evidence of unhappiness with aspects of the Patriot Act.

Libraries also became scenes of resistance to the act. Many librarians had earlier objected to the FBI's Library Awareness Program. They had the same objections to Section 215 of the Patriot Act, which would allow investigators to request records of library patrons' activities and would prevent librarians from revealing that the records had been requested. Many librarians considered spying on patrons' reading habits to be a violation of their profession's ethics and responsibilities. "Protecting the confidentiality of one's use of the library is of primary concern to librarians," said Judith Krug, executive director of the American Library Association's Office for Intellectual Freedom, in 2003.

A few libraries and bookstores adopted a policy of shredding or destroying records earlier than they had previously done, in order to thwart any possible request for a secret review of those records. Other libraries posted signs alerting patrons to the possibility that their reading habits were no longer private. In Santa Cruz, California, for example, signs went up in ten branch libraries and on the library website in 2003. They notified patrons that the library might be forced to turn over records of their reading and computer use to federal agents. The signs advised readers to send their questions about this policy to Attorney General John Ashcroft.

"It's none of their business what anybody's reading," said one Santa Cruz library patron. "It's counterproductive to what libraries are about." Another said, "I'm not reading anything they'd be particularly interested in, but that's not the point. This makes me think of Big Brother."

Because of the gag rule, few details about the FBI's use of library records have emerged. In early 2002 the University of Illinois surveyed 1,023 libraries. Eighty-three libraries reported that law enforcement officials had requested information about patrons, although no details of the requests were revealed. One case that did reach the public unfolded in Washington State several years later. It began when an FBI agent arrived at a small-town library branch and asked for a list of people who had checked out a biography of Osama bin Laden. The request was not accompanied by a national security letter, and the library refused to turn over the information unless the FBI went through legal channels. The FBI

On July 20, 2005, the town of Bristol, Rhode Island, joined the list of communities that had passed resolutions criticizing the Patriot Act. "I'm pleased they passed a resolution," said Nancy Hood. "It went far better than I ever dreamed."

Hood was a member of East Bay Citizens for Peace, a group that opposed both the Iraq War and the Patriot Act. The group had tried several times to convince Bristol's town council to condemn the act completely. The council refused to go that far, because its members recognized the need for the act's security protections. The council did, however, pass a resolution calling on Congress to examine the Patriot Act and change it as needed to protect civil liberties. "The council made it very specific that they did not condemn the act," reported town clerk Louis Cirillo. Instead, the council urged lawmakers to uphold "the fundamental liberties granted to Americans by the Constitution and Bill of Rights."

The resolution, which was sent to members of Congress, said:

> Resolution by the Town of Bristol Reaffirming its Commitment to the U.S. Constitution and its Bill of Rights and Established Freedoms
>
> WHEREAS, the Town Council of Bristol, RI recognizes and upholds the United States Constitution and its Bill of Rights and the Rhode Island Constitution; and WHEREAS, the residents of Bristol cherish their political and civil rights and liberties based upon the Constitution and Bill of Rights; and
>
> WHEREAS, full recognition is taken of the serious nature of the current threats to the United States and its citizens which prompt dynamic

Balancing Act

actions to defend ourselves and our way of life; and

WHEREAS, while we support the necessary thrust of actions for "homeland security," we do not want those actions, directed to preserve our liberties, to in any way abridge the very liberties being defended; and

WHEREAS, the citizens of Bristol, thus, wish to insure that the PATRIOT ACT and related executive orders do not significantly erode our fundamental constitutional protections, including but not limited to due process, the right of privacy, the right to counsel, protection against unreasonable search and seizure and all basic freedoms of the Bill of Rights.

NOW, THEREFORE, BE IT RESOLVED that the Council, while not condemning the PATRIOT ACT, urges its federal delegation to review and work toward revision and/or repeal of those sections of the PATRIOT ACT that may limit or violate the fundamental liberties granted to Americans by the Constitution and Bill of Rights; and

BE IT FURTHER RESOLVED that certified copies of this resolution be transmitted to our Federal Congressional delegates.

responded with a subpoena requesting the records. The library's trustees voted unanimously to go to court to fight the subpoena.

"Our trustees faced a difficult decision," librarian Joan Airoldi later wrote. "It is our job to protect the right of people to obtain the books and other materials they need to form and express ideas. If the government can easily obtain records of the books that our patrons are borrowing, they will not feel free to request the books they want. Who would check out a biography of bin Laden knowing that this might attract the attention of the FBI?"

The FBI withdrew its request, and the matter ended. If the request had been accompanied by a national security letter, however, the library would have had to turn over the records, and Airoldi would have been barred from writing about the incident. She wrote about it in order to express her opinion that the government *does* have a legitimate right to review library records, under certain circumstances and with protection for individuals' privacy—with warrants that require the government to state exactly what records it wants, and why. But the Patriot Act, in Airoldi's opinion, went too far. She wrote, "Our government has always possessed the power to obtain library records, but that power has been subject to safeguards. The Patriot Act eliminated those safeguards and made it impossible for people to ask a judge to rule whether the government needs the information it is after."

The American Library Association and the American Booksellers Association called for changes to the law in order to protect the readers' privacy and their right to read published works, which are constitutionally protected expressions of free speech, without fear. In 2003 Representative Bernie

Sanders of Vermont introduced the Freedom to Read Protection Act to the House of Representatives. The bill, which had the support of civil liberties organizations as well as the librarians' and booksellers' groups, was opposed by House Republicans but eventually passed in June 2005. The bill did not become law, however, because it never came under serious consideration in the Senate. By that time the Senate was deep in debate over the renewal of the Patriot Act.

INTO THE SUNSET?

Sixteen "sunset" provisions of the Patriot Act were set to expire on December 31, 2005. In the spring of that year, Congress began holding hearings on reauthorization, the process by which the nation's legislators would vote on renewing the Patriot Act, with or without changes.

In the years that had passed since the passage of the act, considerable criticism had been leveled at the act, the Department of Justice's enforcement of it, and the Bush administration's conduct of the war on terror. The urgency that lawmakers had felt after 9/11—the pressure to act quickly and to conform to the administration's wishes—had eased. The result was a vigorous congressional debate between those who wanted to change the Patriot Act and those who wanted to leave it alone, or even strengthen it. Most of the debate concerned the controversial sunset provisions. Should these provisions be allowed to expire, or be renewed with a new sunset date, or made permanent parts of the Patriot Act?

The debate hit some rough spots. At one point during a hearing in the House Judiciary Committee, criticism of the Bush administration's domestic surveillance of citizens so angered Republican committee chairman James Sensenbrenner that he walked out, cutting off the hearing in the middle of testimony from Democratic representatives. By July, however, the Republican-dominated House of Representatives had produced a reauthorization bill that largely reflected the desire of the Bush administration and the Justice Department to keep the powers granted by the Patriot Act intact. The Senate, in contrast, produced a bill that eliminated or reformed some of the more controversial provisions. The Senate passed this bill by a unanimous vote in July.

Just as had happened with the original Patriot Act in 2001, the House and Senate versions of the reauthorization bill were sent to a conference committee to be combined into a single bill. The result was a "conference bill" that, some senators felt, had been taken over by the Republicans. On January 31, 2006, on the floor of the Senate, Patrick Leahy of Vermont explained what had happened:

> Every single Senator—Republican and Democratic—voted last July to mend and extend the PATRIOT Act. That bipartisan solution was cast aside by the Bush administration and Republican congressional leaders when they hijacked the conference report, rewrote the bill in ways that fell short of protecting civil liberties and then tried to ram it through Congress as an all-or-nothing proposition. . . . There is no reason why the American people cannot have a PATRIOT Act that is both effective and that adequately protects their rights and their privacy.

The Senate's objection to the conference report meant that Congress had to try again to craft a Patriot Act reauthorization that both houses would accept. The clock was ticking, so both parties agreed to a temporary extension that postponed the expiration of the sunset provisions to the end of January 2006. When that date approached, they agreed to another extension, this time to March 10.

Before the second deadline arrived, the Senate agreed to a compromise bill that was basically a reworking of the conference report bill, as long as a set of Senate amendments could be added to the package. Together these pieces of legislation contained fewer protections for civil liberties than the version of the bill the Senate had passed in July 2005. Yet Democratic senator Richard Durbin of Illinois, one of the senators who agreed to the compromise, although reluctantly, declared that "if you measure it against the original Patriot Act . . . we've made progress toward protecting basic civil liberties."

The legislative package consisted of the USA PATRIOT Improvement and Reauthorization Act of 2005 (H.R. 3199) and the Senate amendment (S. 2271). They reauthorized the original Patriot Act, with these changes:

> Fourteen of the sixteen provisions that had been "sunsetted" in the original act were made permanent; in other words, those parts of the Patriot Act did not expire and would not need to be reauthorized in the future.

> New sunsets of December 31, 2009, were established for Section 206 (roving wiretaps) and Section 215 (access to records). Individuals whose homes or property are searched under "sneak and peek" warrants must be notified of the search within 30 days. Approval of a senior Federal Bureau of Investigation official is needed for a Section 215 order involving library, bookstore, medical, tax, educational, or firearms records. Request

for a Section 215 order for records of a U.S. citizen must include an explanation of why the records are relevant to an investigation.

Someone who receives a Section 215 order may consult an attorney. Someone who receives an order accompanied by a National Security Letter may ask a U.S. district court to set aside or modify the order. A service provider (such as a phone or Internet company) that receives a national security letter may disclose or reveal the fact that the letter was issued, unless investigators certify that such a disclosure may harm a person, an intelligence investigation, or national security. Libraries are exempt from receiving national security letters.

Congress has an increased role in overseeing the Patriot Act-related activities of the Department of Justice and the FISA Court under Section 109, "Enhanced congressional oversight."

In early March 2006, the House of Representatives passed the reauthorization package by a vote of 280 to 138. The Senate passed it by a vote of 89 to 10. The Patriot Act had survived a major challenge, and on March 9 President Bush signed the reauthorization bill into law.

"I applaud the Senate for voting to renew the Patriot Act and overcoming the partisan attempts to block its passage," Bush declared. "The terrorists have not lost the will or the ability to attack us. . . . This bill will allow our law enforcement officials to continue to use the same tools against terrorists that are already used against drug dealers and other criminals, while safeguarding the civil liberties of the American people."

CHAPTER EIGHT

Monitoring the Act

"Does the Patriot Act work? You bet!" wrote former attorney general John Ashcroft, one of the act's creators, in 2006. According to Ashcroft and other supporters, the Patriot Act has achieved its purpose. In late 2005, when the Patriot Act was awaiting reauthorization, Attorney General Alberto Gonzales stated, "The PATRIOT Act has been very effective in helping law enforcement disrupt terrorist cells, prevent terrorist attacks, and prosecute terrorists."

By the beginning of 2010, the United States had not suffered another terrorist attack, despite close calls such as a 2009 attempt to set off explosives on a jet bound for Detroit. No one, however, can guarantee that another attack will not take place. Undoubtedly the Patriot Act has contributed to Americans' safety, but other factors, including luck and the terrorists' resources, abilities, and intentions, must have played a part as well. One sign of the Patriot Act's effectiveness, however, may be the fact that major terrorist attacks

The scene of the Madrid train bombing disaster, claimed in the name of Al-Qaeda.

have occurred in the United Kingdom and in Spain, both of which are Western nations that lack an overall antiterrorism law like the Patriot Act.

Determining the effectiveness of the Patriot Act is difficult, because many actions carried out under the act by Justice Department, intelligence, or law enforcement agents are swathed in secrecy. Information about the operations of the Patriot Act comes primarily from the Justice Department, which makes reports to Congress and also occasionally releases details about specific cases or investigations to the public. Although these reports highlight the successes of the Patriot Act, problems with the act have also made the news. Because the American judicial system allows laws to be challenged, tested, and debated in court, lawsuits have tested the limits of Patriot Act powers.

PATRIOT ACT SUCCESS STORIES

Counterterrorism operations are secret by their very nature. Information about specific investigations carried out under the Patriot Act reaches the public rarely, and only after the investigation has ended. In July of 2004, however, Attorney General John Ashcroft and the Justice Department issued a document titled "Report from the Field: The USA PATRIOT Act at Work." It gave highlights of many cases that showed how law enforcement and intelligence agents had used the provisions of the Patriot Act over the previous few years.

One of the first big successful counterterrorism investigations to gain publicity after 9/11 was the case of the Portland Seven. These were seven men from Portland, Oregon, who had tried in 2001 and 2002 to go to Afghanistan to fight on the side of Al-Qaeda and another radical Islamic group called the Taliban. An undercover informant learned about this group, classified by the Justice Department as a terror cell, from one of its members, Jeffrey Battle, who described plans to bomb Jewish schools and synagogues.

Law enforcement officials faced a hard question. Should they arrest Battle at once and possibly lose the chance to catch the other members of the cell, or wait while they gathered evidence against the others, taking the chance that an anti-Jewish attack would occur while they waited? Provisions of the Patriot Act, however, allowed the Federal Bureau of Investigation to apply for a FISA warrant to keep Battle under surveillance, listening to his telephone conversations and monitoring his Internet use. In this way the investigators expected to learn about any potential attack during the planning stage, when they could take action to stop it. Because Battle did not know that he was under surveillance, though, the investigators continued to gather evidence against the

Cyberterrorism

"I've hacked into the server of your South Pole Research Station," the e-mail message read. "Pay me off, or I will sell the station's data to another country and tell the world how vulnerable you are."

The message arrived at the operations center of the U.S. National Science Foundation in Washington, D.C. The foundation's administrators knew that the message wasn't a hoax, a hacker's crude prank with no basis in fact. It contained data that could only have come from the foundation's own computer systems, which meant that the threat was real. The National Science Foundation was vulnerable—and so was its South Pole station.

The date was May 3, 2003, the start of the Antarctic winter. Temperatures around the South Pole Research Station would soon fall as low as -70° Fahrenheit. Fierce winter weather would make it impossible for aircraft to land at the station before November. Fifty-eight scientists were wintering over at the station, spending the dark, cold months at work on a variety of research projects. The station's life-support systems were controlled by the same National Science Foundation servers that the unknown hacker had penetrated, which meant that the scientists were at grave risk. Someone with access to the servers could manipulate the life-support system, perhaps turning off the heat. Cyberterrorism—which means using the Internet to make a terrorist threat or attack—had struck Antarctica.

The National Science Foundation at once called the Federal Bureau of Investigation. FBI agents went to work under Section 212 of the Patriot Act, which allows companies that provide electronic communications services to reveal their records to law enforcement agents when someone is in immediate danger of death or serious physical injury. Acting under Section 212, investigators traced the e-mail message to a trucking company in Pennsylvania. The hackers had

at the South Pole

used the company's communication system, without the company's knowledge, in an attempt to hide the true origin of the message.

From Pennsylvania the electronic trail led to a cyber-cafe in the Eastern European nation of Romania. The Federal Bureau of Investigation and Romanian police worked together on the case, and on June 3 the investigators arrested two Romanian hackers and seized evidence against them. Fortunately for the Antarctic researchers, in the month that had passed since the threat, no damage had been done to the South Pole Research Station.

other six members of the cell. Six of the men were eventually arrested, tried, and convicted to prison sentences. The seventh managed to get to Pakistan, where he was killed in 2003. Said the Justice Department's report, "Without Sections 218 and 504 of the USA PATRIOT Act, however, this case would likely have been referred to as the 'Portland One' rather than the 'Portland Seven.'"

Section 219 of the Patriot Act allows a federal judge to issue warrants that apply in other jurisdictions, which can save time for investigators, who no longer have to request warrants in each jurisdiction. In 2002, for example, someone in New Jersey accidentally received a package intended for another person. It contained false identification papers. Law enforcement officials traced the sender (in Texas) and the intended receiver (in New Jersey) of the package. Both possessed large stockpiles of weapons, including some illegal items such as chemical weapons and armor-piercing bullets. Under Section 219 of the Patriot Act, the investigators were able to use the New Jersey warrant to search a property in Vermont that belonged to the New Jersey man, rather than obtaining a separate Vermont warrant. This property, too, had a cache of weapons. The investigators felt that their ability to search the Vermont property quickly prevented associates of the suspect from removing the weapons.

Under Section 212 of the Patriot Act, providers of Internet services can disclose confidential customer information to law enforcement in cases where there is an immediate threat of death or serious injury. Investigators used this provision to identify and capture an El Paso, Texas, man who had e-mailed a threat to burn a mosque to the ground.

The Patriot Act has also proven useful in cases that have nothing to do with terrorism. Among the successes cited in the Justice Department's "Report from the Field," for example, are the recovery of an eighty-eight-year-old Wisconsin woman who had been kidnapped and held for ransom, the capture of an armed fugitive in an assault case through the tracing of his e-mails, the uncovering of a child pornography ring on the Internet, and the arrest and conviction of an Indiana man who had sexually abused his daughter and posted pictures of the crime on the Internet. All of these investigations made use of one or more provisions of the Patriot Act. The act even helped bring about the downfall of New York governor Eliot Spitzer in 2008, after a "suspicious activity report" from a bank—a provision of the Patriot Act that was intended to trap money launderers—revealed that Spitzer was transferring large sums of money. The funds, it turned out, were paying for prostitution services, and Spitzer resigned as governor in the midst of a scandal.

CONGRESSIONAL OVERSIGHT

The Patriot Act that Congress passed in 2001 included a number of provisions calling for congressional oversight. The idea was that these provisions would allow Congress to supervise, or at least to review, the activities that federal agents, police, and others would carry out under the Patriot Act.

Section 109 of the reauthorization bill expanded Congress's role in overseeing the use of some of the most controversial parts of the Patriot Act. It required that the Justice Department submit reports to Congress every six months stating how many FISA permits were issued for searches and wiretaps. It also required the Department of Homeland Security to report each year to Congress on the investigations carried out by U.S. Citizenship and Immigration Services. In addition, new and detailed reporting requirements were attached to the specific parts of the act that deal with national security letters, access to records, roving wiretaps, and delayed notification ("sneak and peek") searches.

All of this oversight was meant to keep the Patriot Act within appropriate and legal limits. The lawmakers who had pushed for the oversight provisions hoped that those provisions would ensure that Congress knew what was being done in the name of the Patriot Act. This oversight would therefore prevent the abuses of civil liberties that critics of the act feared. Yet Senator Russ Feingold warned, "Simply requiring reporting on the Government's use of these overly expansive tools does not ensure that they won't be abused."

Reporting requirements mean nothing if they are not followed. President Bush signed the reauthorized Patriot Act into law in front of reporters and guests. Later, after they had left, he quietly added a signing statement to the bill. Such a statement is a document setting forth a president's interpretation of a new law. In Bush's Patriot Act signing statement, he declared that he did not consider himself—or the executive branch of government, which includes the Justice Department—to be bound by the reporting requirements that were built into the law. In the president's view, only the executive branch of government had the power to decide what information it would share with other branches or with the public.

Congress does, however, receive some information about how the Patriot Act is used. As regards civil liberties, the most controversial elements of the act, one source of information is a report issued every six months by the Office of the Inspector General, an independent office within the Justice Department that reports to both the department and Congress. Along with evaluations of problems within the

FBI and other matters, these reports tell how the Office of the Inspector General has handled civil liberties complaints related to the Patriot Act.

The February 2009 report reveals that between July and December of 2008 the Office of the Inspector General received 516 complaints related to civil liberties and the Patriot Act. The office determined that 68 of the complaints did not deserve investigation. Another 270 had to do with agencies outside the Justice Department, such as other federal departments, local governments, or private businesses. The Office of the Inspector General referred these complaints to those agencies.

The office reviewed the remaining 178 complaints. The great majority—170 of the complaints—turned out to be concerned with matters other than civil rights violations under the Patriot Act. These included complaints about prisoners' treatment in federal prisons or complaints that the Justice Department had not investigated an earlier complaint. Of the complaints it did investigate, the office found that most did not appear to involve questions of civil liberties. The Office of the Inspector General sent these complaints to whatever other divisions of the Justice Department had jurisdiction over each type of complaint.

That left eight complaints to be investigated for possible civil rights violations as a result of the Patriot Act. The Office of the Inspector General investigated one of these complaints, which came from a Muslim prisoner in a federal prison. The prisoner claimed that he was punished and persecuted by the prison staff because he had filed a lawsuit against several staff members of the Bureau of Prisons, which oversees federal prisons. During the investigation, the prisoner withdrew both the complaint and the lawsuit, saying that he had made false accusations. The other seven complaints, which also came from Muslim prison inmates or their spouses, were referred to the Bureau of Prisons. Some of the complaints were found to be without substance. Others were still being investigated when the report was issued.

The Office of the Inspector General also reported to Congress that some complaints from earlier periods had been found, upon investigation, to have substance. One inmate from Afghanistan, for example, claimed that Bureau of Prisons staff had insulted him and discriminated against him because of his Afghan origins. The investigation upheld the prisoner's claim, and two prison employees were suspended and disciplined for unprofessional actions. Cases such as this, however, were not directly related to the Patriot Act. The Office of the Inspector General declared to Congress, "None of the 516 complaints we processed during this reporting period specifically alleged misconduct by DOJ employees relating to use of a provision in the Patriot Act."

LEGAL CHALLENGES TO THE PATRIOT ACT

Not all Patriot Act operations have been success stories. Problems and legal challenges have also arisen out of the operations of the act. Aspects of the war on terror that have led to lawsuits include national security letters and the legal status of imprisoned enemy combatants.

National Security Letters

In 2004 the American Civil Liberties Union sued the Department of Justice on behalf of an Internet service provider who had received a national security letter and been warned not to tell anyone about it. The suit charged that the gag order was unconstitutional because it unjustly limited freedom of speech and other protected rights. The following year a group of librarians in Bridgeport, Connecticut, again aided by the American Civil Liberties Union, sued the Justice Department on similar grounds. FBI agents had delivered a national security letter to a librarian, who refused to turn over the records it demanded. The librarians sued for the right to challenge and protest the letter publicly.

In the first case, a federal district court found the use of national security letters under the Patriot Act to be unconstitutional. The Justice Department appealed this decision to a higher court, but the court eventually dropped most elements of the case after the Patriot Act reauthorization. In the Connecticut case, a district court declared that the Justice Department could not enforce the gag order that made disclosing the letter a felony, and the Justice Department agreed to lift the gag order. Civil libertarians hailed both outcomes as victories against the more restrictive provisions of the Patriot Act, although they had little real significance.

More problems for the Patriot Act arose in 2007. In March the Office of the Inspector General released a report that revealed widespread abuse of national security letters. Not only had the FBI issued as many as a thousand such letters that violated Justice Department regulations, but it had done such a poor job of keeping records of the letters that its reports on their use were highly inaccurate.

In September of that same year, in a lawsuit brought against the Justice Department by the American Civil Liberties Union, a federal judge ruled that the FBI's use of national security letters rather than warrants to gain access to telecommunications companies' e-mail and telephone records was unconstitutional. This was because the gag orders associated with the letters violated the First Amendment guarantee of free speech, ruled Judge Victor Marrero. He also ruled that the letters themselves violated the separation of powers created by the Constitution, because the executive branch maintained that it could issue the orders indefinitely, with no review by the judicial branch. Marrero called the secrecy provisions of national security letters "the legislative equivalent of breaking and entering, with an ominous free pass to the hijacking of constitutional values."

The Justice Department appealed Marrero's ruling to a federal appeals court. In December 2008 the appeals court upheld part of Marrero's decision, declaring the use of gag orders with national security letters to be unconstitutional. The court took the position that the government should have to demonstrate why those who receive such letters must be silent, rather than forcing silence on all recipients. Civil libertarians hoped that this ruling would sharply limit the use of national security letters, which had increased dramatically in recent years, from about 9,000 in 2000 to more than 50,000 in 2005.

The Justice Department's problems with the letters, however, were not over. In March 2008 a report from the Office of the Inspector General revealed that in 2006 the FBI had tried to conceal the improper use of national security letters during the previous three years by issuing retroactive subpoenas intended to cover thousands of requests for records from the telecommunications companies Verizon, AT&T, and MCI. The idea was that the subpoenas would take the place of the documentation that the Federal Bureau of Investigation had failed to provide at the time. Glenn Fine, the inspector general who issued the 2008 report, said that although the FBI had made changes in its procedures, "it is too soon to definitively state whether the new systems and controls developed by the Federal Bureau of Investigation and the Department will eliminate fully the problems with the use of NSLs." The question of the gag orders, however, appeared to be settled. In May 2009 the Obama administration announced that it did not plan to ask the Supreme Court to review the federal appeals court's ruling that the gag orders were unconstitutional. The ban on gag orders remained in force.

Detainees' Rights

From the start of the war on terror, questions arose over what rights—if any—were possessed by the enemy combatants who were detained at Guantanamo Bay and in Iraq and Afghanistan. The Bush administration argued that because the detention centers were not located in the United States, people detained in them did not have rights under U.S. law. In particular, the detainees were said not to have the right of habeas corpus, which is the constitutional right of U.S. citizens not to be detained by the government without a specific charge being made against them. Attorneys representing some detainees or their families tested this position by filing habeas corpus requests with the court system, asking that the detainees be either charged with a particular crime or released from wrongful imprisonment. At issue was the question of whether the detainees had the right to make such requests.

In 2004 the case of *Rasul* v. *Bush* became the first of the detainees' habeas corpus cases to reach the U.S. Supreme Court. The Court ruled that the justice system, not the executive branch, has the authority to determine whether noncitizens were being wrongfully held. The Court granted the detainees the right to hear and testify against whatever evidence was being used to hold them. As a result, the Defense

Department established military tribunals, or courts, to hear the cases of the enemy combatants. The Detainee Treatment Act of the following year contained measures that limited the detainees' access to courts and prevented new habeas corpus requests from being filed.

The habeas corpus case of *Hamdan* v. *Rumsfeld* had already entered the justice system when the Detainee Treatment Act was passed. When this case reached the Supreme Court in 2006, the Court ruled that only Congress, not the executive branch, could establish military tribunals to try the non-citizen detainees. A few months later Congress passed the Military Commissions Act. This law authorized the detainee tribunals to continue, and it also called for an end to habeas corpus requests from the detainees.

One such request that was already in the justice system was the case of *Boumediene* v. *Bush*. In 2007 a federal appeals court denied the request, claiming that the detainee Lakhdar Boumediene had no right of habeas corpus, according to the Military Commissions Act. Attorneys for Boumediene and another detainee, Al Odah, appealed the case to the Supreme Court, which agreed to hear it. In 2008 the Court delivered its ruling. By a margin of 5 to 4, the Court found that noncitizen detainees do have the right of habeas corpus under the U.S. Constitution, and that the Military Commission Act had been unconstitutional in depriving them of those rights.

The Supreme Court's ruling in *Boumediene* v. *Bush* meant that detainees could go to court to challenge the grounds on which they were being held. Justice Antonin Scalia, a conservative member of the Supreme Court, had voted against granting habeas corpus rights to the detainees. He declared that "the decision will make the war harder on us. It will almost certainly cause more Americans to be killed." Justice

Anthony Kennedy, who had voted for granting the rights, pointed out that "[t]he laws and Constitution are designed to survive, and remain in force, in extraordinary times." And President Bush, who was disappointed with the decision, announced, "It's a Supreme Court decision. We will abide by the decision." The legal status of the detainees had been tested and established in the courts of law, like other provisions of the Patriot Act. That process of questioning and testing may continue as long as the act remains in force.

THE FUTURE OF THE PATRIOT ACT

For many of its supporters and its critics, the Patriot Act is forever linked to the administration of President George W. Bush and to his attorney general, John Ashcroft. When Bush's presidency ended in January 2009 and Barack Obama, a Democrat, took office as the nation's new leader, some wondered whether the change in administration might bring changes in the Patriot Act. Obama had already announced that he would make some changes in the way the war on terror was being waged, such as closing the detention center for enemy combatants at Guantanamo Bay. It is possible that during Obama's presidency Congress will again consider changes to the Patriot Act. No one expects the act to be revoked, or cancelled, in its entirety. Terrorism remains a real and serious threat, and both law enforcement and intelligence officials, as well as those who guide the nation, are called upon to stand as a shield against it.

Perhaps only future historians will be able to see clearly how successfully the Patriot Act has safeguarded the United States and its citizens, or whether the act brought about an erosion of America's values and civil liberties, or both. Those who fought for the act, however, have no doubts about

Many hoped that the election of President Barack Obama would lead to changes in the Patriot Act, and how the war on terror was fought. Obama has pledged to close the prison at Guantanamo Bay, but, as of spring 2010, no one has been willing to take in those prisoners.

that question. In the words of President Bush in 2005, "The Patriot Act has accomplished exactly what it was designed to do—it has protected American liberty, and saved American lives." Those who oppose the Patriot Act, however, fear that it strikes at the very freedoms that define America.

Chronology

2001 September 11: Terrorists in hijacked airplanes attack New York City and Washington, D.C., landmarks

September 19: Congress, White House, and Department of Justice meet to discuss proposals for antiterrorism law

October 11: Senate passes USA Act, S. 1510, 96–1

October 12: House passes PATRIOT Act, H.R. 2975, 337–79

October 23: USA PATRIOT Act, H.R. 3162, which incorporates the two earlier acts, is introduced in House of Representatives

October 24: House passes USA PATRIOT Act, 357–66

October 25: Senate passes USA PATRIOT Act, 98–1

October 26: President George W. Bush signs USA PATRIOT Act (known as Patriot Act) into law

2004–2005 U.S. District Court upholds legal challenge to Patriot Act use of national security letters and gag orders

2006 Two bills reauthorize Patriot Act and eliminate all but two of its sunset provisions

2007 Federal appeals court rules national security letter gag orders unconstitutional

2008 Federal Bureau of Investigation misuse of subpoenas to cover Patriot Act abuses is revealed; Supreme Court rules in *Boumediene* v. *Bush* that detainees have the right of habeas corpus

2009 Obama administration wants to extend roving wiretaps and other controversial act provisions, as well as indefinite detention of some detainees; other detainees will be tried or imprisoned in the United States

From Bill to Law

For a proposal to become a federal law, it must go through many steps:

In Congress:

1. A bill is proposed by a citizen, a legislator, the president, or another interested party. Most bills originate in the House and then are considered in the Senate.

2. A representative submits the bill to the House (the first reading). A senator submits it to the Senate. The person (or people) who introduces the bill is its main sponsor. Other lawmakers can become sponsors to show support for the bill. Each bill is read three times before the House or the Senate.

3. The bill is assigned a number and referred to the committee(s) and subcommittee(s) dealing with the topic. Each committee adopts its own rules, following guidelines of the House and the Senate. The committee chair controls scheduling for the bill.

4. The committees hold hearings if the bill is controversial or complex. Experts and members of the public may testify. Congress may compel witnesses to testify if they do not do so voluntarily.

5. The committee reviews the bill, discusses it, adds amendments, and makes other changes it deems necessary during markup sessions.

6. The committee votes on whether to support the bill, oppose it, or take no action on it and issues a report on its findings and recommendations.

7. A bill that receives a favorable committee report goes to the Rules Committee to be scheduled for consideration by the full House or Senate.

8. If the committee delays a bill or if the Rules Committee fails to schedule it, House members can sign a discharge motion and call for a vote on the matter. If a majority votes to release the bill from committee, it is scheduled on the calendar as any other bill would be. Senators may vote to discharge the bill from a committee as well. More commonly, though, a senator will add the bill as an amendment to an unrelated bill in order to get it past the committee blocking it. Or a senator can request that a bill be put directly on the Senate calendar, where it will be scheduled for debate. House and Senate members can also vote to suspend the rules and vote directly on a bill. Bills passed in this way must receive support from two thirds of those voting.

9. Members of both houses debate the bill. In the House, a chairperson moderates the discussion and each speaker's time is limited. Senators can speak on the issue for as long as they wish. Senators who want to block the bill may debate for hours in a tactic known as a filibuster. A three-fifths vote of the Senate is required to stop the filibuster (cloture), and talk on the bill is then limited to one hour per senator.

10. Following the debate, the bill is read section by section (the second reading). Members may propose amendments, which are voted on before the final bill comes up for a vote.

11. The full House and Senate then debate the entire bill and those amendments approved previously. Debate continues until a majority of members vote to "move the previous question" or approve a special resolution forcing a vote.

12. A full quorum—at least 218 members in the House, 51 in the Senate—must be present for a vote to be held. A member may request a formal count of members to ensure a quorum is on hand. Absent members are sought when there is no quorum.

13. Before final passage, opponents are given a last chance to propose amendments that alter the bill; the members vote on them.

14. A bill needs approval from a majority of those voting to pass. Members who do not want to take a stand on the issue may choose to abstain (not vote at all) or merely vote present.

15. If the House passes the bill, it goes on to the Senate. By that time, bills often have more than one hundred amendments attached to them. Occasionally, a Senate bill will go to the House.

16. If the bill passes in the same form in both the House and the Senate, it is sent to the clerk to be recorded.

17. If the Senate and the House version differ, the Senate sends the bill to the House with the request that members approve the changes.

18. If the two houses disagree on the changes, the bill may go to conference, where members appointed by the House and the Senate work out a compromise if possible.

19. The House and the Senate vote on the revised bill agreed to in conference. Further amendments may be added and the process repeated if the Senate and the House version of the bill differ.

20. The bill goes to the president for a signature.

To the President:

1. If the president signs the bill, it becomes law.

2. If the president vetoes the bill, it goes back to Congress, which can override his veto with a two-thirds vote in both houses.

3. If the president takes no action, the bill automatically becomes law after ten days if Congress is still in session.

4. If Congress adjourns and the president has taken no action on the bill within ten days, it does not become law. This is known as a pocket veto.

The time from introduction of the bill to the signing can range from several months to the entire two-year session. If a bill does not win approval during the session, it can be reintroduced in the next Congress, where it will have to go through the whole process again.

Notes

Chapter One

p. 7, "A plane has crashed . . .": Robert O'Harrow Jr., "Six Weeks in Autumn," *Washington Post Magazine*, October 27, 2002, www.washingtonpost.com/wp-dyn/content/article/2006/05/09/AR2006050900961.html

p. 9, "The guy [pilot] . . .": Dan Balz and Bob Woodward, "America's Chaotic Road to War," *Washington Post*, January 27, 2002, www.washingtonpost.com/wp-dyn/articles/A42754-2002Jan26.html

p. 9, "A second plane . . .": Balz and Woodward, "America's Chaotic Road to War," January 27, 2002.

p. 9, "They had declared war . . ." Balz and Woodward, "America's Chaotic Road to War," January 27, 2002.

p. 9, "'Sir,' Tenet told the president, 'I believe it's . . .'": Herbert Foerstel, *The Patriot Act: A Documentary and Reference Guide*, Westport, CT: Greenwood, 2008, 26.

p. 10, "This has bin Laden . . .": Balz and Woodward, "America's Chaotic Road to War," January 27, 2002.

p. 10, "a series of deliberate . . .": George W. Bush, address to the nation, Washington, DC: National Center for Public Policy Research, September 11, 2001, www.nationalcenter.org/BushGW91101Address.html

pp. 10–11, "The Pearl Harbor of the 21st century . . .": Balz and Woodward, "America's Chaotic Road to War," January 27, 2002.

p. 12, "Congress will convene tomorrow . . .": Tom Daschle, public address, quoted in Foerstel, *The Patriot Act*, 25.

p. 13, "all that is necessary . . .": O'Harrow, "Six Weeks in Autumn," October 27, 2002.

Chapter Two

pp. 15–16, "It is important . . .": John Ashcroft, *Never Again: Securing America and Restoring Justice*, New York: Center Street, 2006, 141–142.

p. 17, "I was just thinking . . .": Robert O'Harrow Jr., "Six Weeks in Autumn," *Washington Post Magazine*, October 27, 2002, www.washingtonpost.com/wp-dyn/content/article/2006/05/09/AR2006050900961.html

p. 18, "It is essential . . .": Orrin Hatch and Jon Kyl, quoted in Declan McCullagh, "Senate OKs Federal Bureau of Investigation Net Spying," *Wired*, September 14, 2001, www.wired.com/politics/law/news/2001/09/46852

p. 19, "Maybe the Senate . . .": McCullagh, "Senate OKs Federal Bureau of Investigation Net Spying," September 14, 2001.

p. 20, "I saw the same shock . . .": O'Harrow, "Six Weeks in Autumn," October 27, 2002.

p. 20, "knee-jerk reaction . . .": O'Harrow, "Six Weeks in Autumn," October 27, 2002.

p. 21, "There can be no doubt . . .": O'Harrow, "Six Weeks in Autumn," October 27, 2002.

p. 22, "I had never seen . . .": O'Harrow, "Six Weeks in Autumn," October 27, 2002.

p. 22, "We must have faith . . .": O'Harrow, "Six Weeks in Autumn," October 27, 2002.

p. 22, "more than 150 organizations . . .": Christopher M. Finan, *From the Palmer Raids to the Patriot Act: A History of the Fight for Free Speech in America*, Boston: Beacon Press, 2007, 279.

p. 22, "we were going to have another . . .": O'Harrow, "Six Weeks in Autumn," October 27, 2002.

p. 23, "In order to curb terrorism in . . .": *Los Angeles Times*, September 13–14, 2001, poll, quoted in Amitai Etzioni, *How Patriotic Is the Patriot Act?*, New York: Routledge, 2004, 19.

Chapter Three

p. 25, "a different kind of conflict . . .": George W. Bush, "President's Radio Address," September 15, 2001, www.pbs.org/newshour/bb/military/terroristattack/radio-address_9-15.html

pp. 26–27, "Both versions . . .": Robert O'Harrow Jr., "Six Weeks in Autumn," *Washington Post Magazine*, October 27, 2002, www.washingtonpost.com/wp-dyn/content/article/2006/05/09/AR2006050900961.html

p. 27, "One key feature of the compromise . . .": Herbert Foerstel, *The Patriot Act: A Documentary and Reference Guide*, Westport, CT: Greenwood, 2008, 33.

pp. 27–28, "According to one senator . . .": Russ Feingold, interview by Matthew Rothschild, *The Progressive*, May 2002, 32.

p. 28, "News reports at the time . . .": *Online NewsHour*, "Ashcroft Urges Swift Passage of Anti-Terrorism Bill," October 3, 2001, www.pbs.org/newshour/updates/october01/anti-terror_10-3.html

p. 28, "I think it is time . . .": John Ashcroft and Orrin Hatch, quoted in Christopher M. Finan, *From the Palmer Raids to the Patriot Act: A History of the Fight for Free Speech in America*, Boston: Beacon Press, 2007, 277.

p. 29, "a more balanced Patriot Act bill . . .": Foerstel, *The Patriot Act*, 33.

pp. 30–31, "There is no doubt . . .": Russ Feingold, quoted in 107th Cong., 1st sess., *Congressional Record 136*, October 11, 2001, S10570, http://frwebgate.access.gpo.gov/cgi-bin/getpage.cgi?position=all&page=S10570&dbname=2001_record

p. 31, "to protect individual liberties . . .": Feingold, quoted in *Congressional Record 136*, October 11, 2001, S10570.

p. 31, "the very delicate balance . . .": Tom Daschle, quoted in *Congressional Record 136*, October 11, 2001, S10574.

p. 31, "I can tell you right now . . .": Patrick Leahy, quoted in *Congressional Record 136*, October 11, 2001, S10575.

p. 32, "a low point for me . . .": Feingold, interview by Matthew Rothschild, 32.

"What you need to know . . .": John Conyers, quoted in Foerstel, *The Patriot Act*, 32.

pp. 32–33, "While the Committee on the Judiciary . . .": Louise Slaughter, quoted in 107th Cong., 1st sess., *Congressional Record 137*, October 12, 2001, H6706, http://frwebgate.access.gpo.gov/cgi-bin/getpage.cgi?position=all&page=H6706&dbname=2001_record

p. 33, "What we have before us . . .": John Conyers, quoted in *Congressional Record 137*, October 12, 2001, H6707.

p. 33, "did not ignore constitutional questions . . .": Conyers, quoted in Foerstel, *The Patriot Act*, 32.

p. 33, "some very, very specific problems . . .": Peter Deutsch, quoted in *Congressional Record 137*, October 12, 2001, H6707.

p. 34, "Senate passage of this measure . . .": Patrick Leahy, "Statement of Senator Patrick Leahy, Chairman, Senate Judiciary Committee, and Democratic Manager of the Senate Debate on the Anti-Terrorism Bill," October 25, 2001, http://leahy.senate.gov/press/200110/102501.html

pp. 34–35, "This was not the . . .": Leahy, "Statement of Senator Patrick Leahy," October 25, 2001.

p. 35, "a far better bill . . .": Leahy, "Statement of Senator Patrick Leahy," October 25, 2001.

p. 35, "This legislation is essential . . .": George W. Bush, quoted in Foerstel, *The Patriot* Act, 47.

Chapter Four

p. 40, "for the mutual preservation of their lives . . .": John Locke, *The Second Treatise of Civil Government*, 6th ed., 1764, web ed., ebooks@Adelaide, http://ebooks.adelaide.edu.au/l/locke/john/l81s/chapter9.html

p. 41, "separate and equal . . .": U.S. Congress, Declaration of Independence, July 4, 1776, College Park, MD: U.S. National Archives and Records Administration, www.archives.gov/exhibits/charters/declaration_transcript.html

p. 42, "the right of the people to be . . .": U.S. Constitution, Bill of Rights, College Park, MD: U.S. National Archives and Records Administration, www.archives.gov/exhibits/charters/bill_of_rights_transcript.html

p. 43, "No State shall make or enforce . . .": U.S. Constitution, Amendments, College Park, MD: U.S. National Archives and Records Administration, www.archives.gov/exhibits/charters/constitution_amendments_11-27.html

p. 44, "*Silent enim leges . . .*": Marcus Tullius Cicero, "Pro T. Annio Milone," *Oxford Companion to Classical Literature*, Oxford: Oxford University Press, 1993, www.uah.edu/society/texts/latin/classical/cicero/promilone1.html

p. 47, "Like a prairie-fire . . .": A. Mitchell Palmer, "The Case Against the Reds," *Forum* 64, 1920, 173–185, http://chnm.gmu.edu/courses/hist409/palmer.html

p. 48, "The people who were arrested . . .": Christopher M. Finan, *From the Palmer Raids to the Patriot Act: A History of the Fight for Free Speech in America*, Boston: Beacon Press, 2007, 3.

p. 50, "Aboard were 249 prisoners . . .": Finan, *From the Palmer Raids to the Patriot Act*, 5.

pp. 50–51, "Ever since I have been in this country . . .": Emma Goldman, quoted in Finan, *From the Palmer Raids to the Patriot Act*, 4–5.

Chapter Five

p. 53, "The 9/11 attacks occurred on a Tuesday . . .": John Ashcroft, *Never Again: Securing America and Restoring Justice*, New York: Center Street, 2006, 154.

p. 54, "In reality, the Patriot Act . . .": Herbert N. Foerstel, *The Patriot Act: A Documentary and Reference Guide*, Westport, CT: Greenwood, 2008, 30.

p. 54, "In the decades prior to 9/11 . . .": Ashcroft, *Never Again*, 144–154.

p. 56, "Hoover's list consisted of . . .": Tim Weiner, "Hoover Planned Mass Jailing in 1950," *New York Times*, December 23, 2007, www.nytimes.com/2007/12/23/washington/23habeas.html?_r=1&adxnnl=1&adxnnlx=1229436440-mUp+f8tSsakWdl81svedmg

p. 58, "the Church Committee . . .": "The Church Committee and FISA," *Bill Moyers Journal*, PBS, October 26, 2007, www.pbs.org/moyers/journal/10262007/profile2.html

p. 58, "Some of the volumes . . .": Frank Church, quoted in Foerstel, *The Patriot Act*, 123.

p. 59, "Between 1953 and 1973, . . .": Robert O'Harrow Jr., "Six Weeks in Autumn," *Washington Post Magazine*, October 27, 2002, www.washingtonpost.com/wp-dyn/content/article/2006/05/09/AR2006050900961.html

p. 60, "The most notorious . . .": Patrick Leahy, "Statement of Senator Patrick Leahy, Chairman, Senate Judiciary Committee, and Democratic Manager of the Senate Debate on the Anti-Terrorism Bill," October 25, 2001, http://leahy.senate.gov/press/200110/102501.html

p. 61, "Much of the government's experience . . .": Leahy, "Statement of Senator Patrick Leahy," October 25, 2001.

p. 62, "Too many people have been spied on . . .": Senate Select Subcommittee to Study Governmental Operations with Respect to Intelligence, quoted in O'Harrow, "Six Weeks in Autumn," October 27, 2002.

p. 62, "The law recognized . . .": Christopher M. Finan, *From the Palmer Raids to the Patriot Act: A History of the Fight for Free Speech in America*, Boston: Beacon Press, 2007, 275.

p. 63, "FISA court . . .": "The Church Committee and FISA," *Bill Moyers Journal*, October 26, 2007.

p. 64, "to conduct electronic surveillance . . .": Brian A. Benczkowski, letter to House Speaker Nancy Pelosi, April 30, 2008, www.fas.org/irp/agency/doj/fisa/2007rept.pdf

p. 65, "wall between government departments . . .": Ashcroft, *Never Again*, 150.

p. 65, "Someday someone will die . . .": Ashcroft, *Never Again*, 151–152.

p. 66, "a big maybe . . .": Ashcroft, *Never Again*, 152.

p. 66, "report anyone . . .": Foerstel, *The Patriot Act*, 4.

p. 67, "report on who was reading what . . .": Foerstel, *The Patriot Act*, 2.

p. 67, "The FBI's request . . .": Foerstel, *The Patriot Act*, 2.

p. 68, "someone lurking around here . . .": Foerstel, *The Patriot Act*, 3.

p. 69, "the Nazi regime, and in Soviet Russia . . .": Fred Lerner, *Libraries Through the Ages*, New York: Continuum, 1999, 105–106.

Chapter Six

pp. 72–83, "The Patriot Act begins . . .": *USA Patriot Act of 2001*, Public Law 107–56, 107th Cong., October 26, 2001, http://frwebgate.access.gpo.gov/cgi-bin/getdoc.cgi?dbname=107 _cong_public_laws&docid=f:publ056.107.pdf

p. 83, "The bill before me . . .": George W. Bush, quoted in Herbert N. Foerstel, *The Patriot Act: A Documentary and Reference Guide*, Westport, CT: Greenwood, 2008, 47.

Chapter Seven

pp. 87–88, "the Bush administration's curtailment . . .": Elaine Cassel, *The War on Civil Liberties: How Bush and Ashcroft Have Dismantled the Bill of Rights*, Chicago: Lawrence Hill Books, 2004, xvi.

p. 89, "Zacarias Moussaoui . . .": Larry Abramson and Maria Godoy, "The Patriot Act: Key Controversies," NPR, December 16, 2005, www.npr.org/news/specials/patriotact/patriot actdeal.html#issue1

p. 89, "Section 218 . . .": John Podesta, "The USA Patriot Act: The Good, the Bad and the Ugly," *American Bar Association Human Rights Magazine*, Winter 2002, www.abanet.org/irr/hr/ winter02/podesta.html

p. 91, "88 percent . . .": "The Patriot Act: Where It Stands," American Civil Liberties Union, http://action.aclu.org/reformthepatriotact/whereitstands.html

pp. 91–92, "the Supreme Court concluded . . .": James B. Comey, quoted in Paul Rosenzweig et al., eds., *The Patriot Act Reader*, Washington, DC: Heritage Foundation, 2004, 11, www. heritage.org/Research/HomelandDefense/upload/69895_1.pdf

p. 93, "allows American citizens to declare . . .": Coleen Rowly, quoted in Herbert N. Foerstel, *The Patriot Act: A Documentary and Reference Guide*, Westport, CT: Greenwood, 2008, 94.

p. 93, "The vast majority . . .": Foerstel, *The Patriot Act*, 106.

p. 93, "You are not an American . . .": Foerstel, *The Patriot Act*, 100.

p. 95, "Lawful combatants receive prisoner of . . .": William Haynes to Members of the ASIL-CFR Roundtable, "Enemy Combatants" memorandum, December 12, 2002, www.cfr.org/ publication/5312/enemy_combatants.html

p. 96, "more than 500 such detainees had been released . . .": "Free at Last," *Time*, June 29, 2009, 10.

p. 98, "The facts of the case . . .": Tim Reid, "Torture Memo Has Put US in Danger, CIA Tells Barack Obama," *Times Online*, April 21, 2009, www.timesonline.co.uk/tol/news/world/ us_and_americas/article6135965.ece

p. 98, "denied that useful . . .": James Gordon Meek, "U.S. Officials Slam Dick Cheney's Claim that Waterboarding 9/11 Mastermind 183 Times Was 'A Success,'" *Daily News*, April 22, 2009, www.nydailynews.com/news/us_world/2009/04/22/2009-04-22_dick_cheney_full _of_crap_official.html

p. 99, "the torture of the ignorant . . .": Darius Rejali, "5 Myths About Torture and Truth,"

Washington Post, December 16, 2007, www.washingtonpost.com/wp-dyn/content/article
/2007/12/13/AR2007121301303.html

p. 99, "irresponsible expressions of opinion . . .": "The Excluded: Ideological Exclusion
and the War on Ideas," American Civil Liberties Union, www.aclu.org/pdfs/safefree/the_
excluded_report.pdf

p. 100, "gutted ideological exclusion . . .": James R. Edwards Jr., "Keeping Extremists Out:
The History of Ideological Exclusion and the Need for Its Revival," Center for Immigration
Studies, September 2005, www.cis.org/articles/2005/back1005.html

p. 100, "Nelson Mandela . . .": "Ideological Exclusion," American Civil Liberties Union, www.
aclu.org/safefree/exclusion/passports_act/

pp. 100–101, "Tariq Ramadan . . .": Christine Kearney, "Obama Lawyer Sticks to Ban on
Muslim Scholar," *Reuters*, March 24, 2009, www.reuters.com/article/domesticNews/idUS-
TRE52N6JT20090324

p. 101, "The First Amendment does not guarantee . . .": Edwards, "Keeping Extremists Out,"
September 2005.

p. 101, "The suggestion that . . .": Brief for Amicus Curiae 08-0826-CV, United States Court
of Appeals, 2nd Cir., May 5, 2008, www.ncac.org/ncacimages/FiledBriefSecondCircuit.pdf

p. 102, "resolutions and ordinances . . .": "Resolutions and Ordinances Critical of the USA
PATRIOT Act and Other Laws and Policies that Diminish Civil Liberties," Bill of Rights
Defense Committee, October 23, 2008, www.bordc.org/resolutions.pdf

p. 103, "Protecting the confidentiality . . .": Judith Krug, quoted in Foerstel, *The Patriot Act*,
150.

p. 103, "It's none of their business . . .": Bob Egelko et al., "Libraries Post Patriot Act Warn-
ings," *SFGate*, March 10, 2003, www.sfgate.com/cgi-bin/article.cgi?f=/c/a/2003/03/10/
MN14634.DTL

p. 103, "Eighty-three libraries . . .": Marti Kasindorg, "FBI's Reading List Worries Librarians,"
USA Today, December 16, 2002, www.usatoday.com/news/nation/2002-12-16-librarians-
usat_x.htm

p. 104, "I'm pleased they passed . . .": Stephen V. Martino, "Bristol Passes Patriot Act
Resolution," *EastBayRI.com*, August 8, 2005, http://ebypublish.bits.baseview.com/story/
336622830080680.php

pp. 104–105, "Resolution by the Town . . .": "Community Resolution for Bristol, RI," American Civil Liberties Union, www.aclu.org/safefree/resources/20290res20050823.html

p. 106, "Our trustees faced a difficult decision . . .": Joan Airoldi, "Librarian's Brush with
Federal Bureau of Investigation Shapes Her View of the USA Patriot Act," *USA Today*, June
17, 2005, www.usatoday.com/news/opinion/editorials/2005-05-17-librarian-edit_x.htm

p. 106, "Our government has always . . .": Airoldi, "Librarian's Brush with Federal Bureau of
Investigation Shapes Her View of the USA Patriot Act," June 17, 2005.

pp. 107–108, "Sensenbrenner that he walked . . .": Foerstel, *The Patriot Act*, 179–180.

p. 108, "Every single senator . . .": Patrick Leahy, quoted in Foerstel, *The Patriot Act*, 180,
181.

p. 109, "if you measure it against . . .": Richard Durbin, quoted in Foerstel, *The Patriot Act*,
181.

p. 109, "They reauthorized . . .": *USA Patriot Improvement and Reauthorization Act of 2005*,
Public Law 109-177, 109th Cong., March 9, 2006, http://frwebgate.access.gpo.gov/cgi-bin/
getdoc.cgi?dbname=109_cong_public_laws&docid=f:publ177.109.pdf

p. 110, "I applaud . . .": "House Approves Patriot Act Renewal," *CNN.com*, March 7, 2006,
www.cnn.com/2006/POLITICS/03/07/patriot.act/

Chapter Eight
p. 111, "Does the Patriot Act work? . . .": John Ashcroft, *Never Again: Securing America and
Restoring Justice*, New York: Center Street, 2006, 155.

p. 111, "The PATRIOT Act has been very effective . . .": Alberto Gonzales, "Gonzales Discusses Patriot Act," transcript, *Washington Post*, December 14, 2005, www.washingtonpost.com/wp-dyn/content/discussion/2005/12/13/DI2005121301425.html

p. 113, "It gave highlights of many cases . . .": "Report from the Field: The USA Patriot Act at Work," Department of Justice, July 2004, http://www.usdoj.gov/olp/pdf/patriot_report_from_the_field0704.pdf

pp. 114–115, "Cyberterrorism at the South Pole": "Report from the Field," Department of Justice, 27; "Testimony of Keith Lourdeau, Deputy Assistant Director, Cyber Division, Federal Bureau of Investigation, Before the Senate Judiciary Subcommittee on Terrorism, Technology, and Homeland Security," Federal Bureau of Investigation, February 24, 2004, http://www.fbi.gov/congress/congress04/lourdeau022404.htm

p. 116, "Without Sections 218 and 504 . . .": "Report from the Field," Department of Justice, July 2004.

pp. 116–117, "Among the successes cited . . .": "Report from the Field," Department of Justice, July 2004.

p. 117, "Eliot Spitzer . . .": Mark Hosenball and Michael Isikoff, "Unintended Consequences," *Newsweek*, March 24, 2008, www.newsweek.com/id/123489

p. 118, "Simply requiring reporting . . .": Russ Feingold, quoted in Herbert N. Foerstel, *The Patriot Act: A Documentary and Reference Guide*, Westport, CT: Greenwood, 2008, 200.

p. 118, "In the president's view, . . .": Charlie Savage, "Bush Shuns Patriot Act Requirement," *The Boston Globe*, March 24, 2006, http://www.boston.com/news/nation/washington/articles/2006/03/24/bush_shuns_patriot_act_requirement/

p. 120, "None of the 516 complaints . . .": "Report to Congress on Implementation of Section 1001 of the USA Patriot Act," Office of the Inspector General, February 2009, 5, www.usdoj.gov/oig/special/s0902/final.pdf

p. 121, "More problems for the Patriot Act . . .": Richard B. Schmitt, "Patriot Act Has Setback in Court," *Los Angeles Times*, September 7, 2007, http://articles.latimes.com/2007/sep/07/nation/na-patriot7

p. 121, "In September . . .": Dan Eggen, "Judge Invalidates Patriot Act Provisions," *Washington Post*, September 7, 2007, A01, www.washingtonpost.com/wp-dyn/content/article/2007/09/06/AR2007090601438.html

p. 122, "the legislative equivalent of breaking and entering . . .": Eggen, "Judge Invalidates Patriot Act Provisions," September 7, 2007.

p. 122, "In December 2008 . . .": Ateqah Khaki, "Blog of Rights: Victory in Patriot Act Case!" American Civil Liberties Union, December 16, 2008, http://blog.aclu.org/2008/12/16/victory-in-patriot-act-case/

pp. 122–123, "it is too soon to definitively state . . .": Ryan Singel, "FBI Tried to Cover Patriot Act Abuses with Flawed, Retroactive Subpoenas, Audit Finds," *Wired*, March 13, 2008, http://www.wired.com/threatlevel/2008/03/fbi-tried-to-co/

p. 124, "Detainee Treatment Act . . .": Judith Resnik, "Opening the Door: Court Stripping: Unconscionable and Unconstitutional?" *Slate*, February 1, 2006, www.slate.com/id/2135240/

p. 124, "Scalia, a conservative member . . .": Jan Crawford Greenburg and Ariane de Vogue, "Supreme Court: Guantanamo Detainees Have Rights in Court," *ABC News Internet*, June 12, 2008, http://abcnews.go.com/print?id=5048935

pp. 125–126, "The Patriot Act has accomplished . . .": George W. Bush, "President Discusses Patriot Act," news release, Office of the Press Secretary, June 9, 2005, http://merln.ndu.edu/archivepdf/hls/WH/20050609-2.pdf

All websites accessible as of August 26, 2009.

Further Information

BOOKS
Ball, Howard. *The USA PATRIOT Act: A Reference Handbook*. Oxford, UK: ABC-CLIO, 2004.

Etzioni, Amitai and Jason H. Marsh, eds. *Rights vs. Public Safety After 9/11*. Lanham, MD: Rowman & Littlefield, 2003.

Gerdes, Louise I., ed. *The Patriot Act*. Farmington Hills, MI: Greenhaven, 2005.

Haugen, David, ed. *National Security*. Farmington Hills, MI: Greenhaven, 2007.

Marcovitz, Harold. *Privacy Rights and the Patriot Act*. Edina, MN: ABDO, 2008.

Miller, Debra. *The Patriot Act*. Farmington Hills, MI: Lucent, 2007.

Nakaya, Andrea C. *America's Battle Against Terrorism*. Farmington Hills, MI: Greenhaven, 2005.

Perl, Lila. *Terrorism*. New York: Marshall Cavendish Benchmark, 2004.

Scheppler, Bill. *The USA PATRIOT Act: Antiterror Legislation in Response to 9/11*. New York: Rosen, 2005.

Stefoff, Rebecca. *Security v. Privacy*. New York: Marshall Cavendish Benchmark, 2008.

Torr, James D. *The Patriot Act*. Farmington Hills, MI: Lucent, 2005.

WEBSITES
www.aclu.org/safefree/index.html
On its "Safe and Free" page the American Civil Liberties Union (ACLU) posts articles about the Patriot Act and the Foreign Intelligence Surveillance Act, focusing on the acts' conflicts with civil liberties. The ACLU has led legal challenges to provisions of the acts.

www.aei.org
The website of the conservative American Enterprise Institute has archived a number of articles about the Patriot Act, including "The Patriot Act and Civil Liberties," "The Patriot Act Under Fire," and "Are We Safer?"

www.dhs.gov/xnews/releases/press_release_0815.shtm
The Department of Homeland Security's "Fact Sheet: The Patriot Act" page lists numerous cases in which law enforcement officials have used the Patriot Act against people involved in illegal money transfers.

www.fas.org/irp/agency/doj/fisa/
The Department of Justice's FISA page is an archive of government documents about the Foreign Intelligence Surveillance Act, including annual reports to Congress and legal challenges.

www.heritage.org/Research/HomelandSecurity/wm612.cfm
The conservative Heritage Foundation, which supports the Patriot Act, offers articles about the Patriot Act and national security. "The Patriot Act Reader: Understanding the Law's Role in the Global War on Terrorism" interprets the major provisions of the act.

www.lifeandliberty.gov/index.html
The Department of Justice maintains this site devoted to the Patriot Act and the Protect America Act. Features include the full texts of both acts, an archive of articles and presidential statements, and "Dispelling the Myths" pages that offer responses to objections to and criticisms of the acts.

www.npr.org/news/specials/patriotact/patriotactdeal.html
National Public Radio's "The Patriot Act: Key Controversies" site presents brief arguments for and against various parts of the Patriot Act, including roving wiretaps and FISA warrants.

www.pbs.org/newshour/extra/features/july-dec03/patriotact_ 9-17.html
This site, a companion to an episode of the PBS program *NewsHour*, provides students with an overview of the Patriot Act and controversies surrounding it.

www.npr.org/templates/story/story.php?storyId=4759727& sourceCode=gaw
National Public Radio's "Debating the Patriot Act" site is an archive of NPR stories about the Patriot Act, representing various points of view.

www.pbs.org/wgbh/pages/frontline/shows/sleeper/tools/patriot.html
This site, a companion to the PBS *Frontline* episode "Chasing the Sleeper Cell," reviews the history of the Patriot Act through 2004.

http://w2.eff.org/patriot/
http://epic.org/privacy/terrorism/usapatriot/
The Electronic Frontier Foundation (EFF) and the Electronic Privacy Information Center (EPIC) view certain provisions of the Patriot Act as threats to civil liberties and privacy, particularly Internet privacy; the organizations maintain these pages about the act and legal challenges to it.

Bibliography

Ashcroft, John. *Never Again: Securing America and Restoring Justice.* New York: Center Street, 2006.

Baker, Stewart A. *Patriot Debates: Experts Debate the USA PATRIOT Act.* Chicago: American Bar Association, 2005.

Brasch, Walter M. *America's Unpatriotic Acts: The Federal Government's Violation of Constitutional and Civil Rights.* New York: Peter Lang, 2005.

Cassel, Elaine. *The War on Civil Liberties: How Bush and Ashcroft Have Dismantled the Bill of Rights.* Chicago: Lawrence Hill Books, 2004.

Etzioni, Amitai. *How Patriotic Is the Patriot Act?* New York: Routledge, 2004.

Finan, Christopher M. *From the Palmer Raids to the Patriot Act: A History of the Fight for Free Speech in America.* Boston: Beacon Press, 2007.

Foerstel, Herbert N. *The Patriot Act: A Documentary and Reference Guide.* Westport, CT: Greenwood, 2008.

———. *Refuge of a Scoundrel: The Patriot Act in Libraries.* Westport, CT: Greenwood, 2004.

Rosenzweig, Paul, Alane Kochems, and James Jay Carafano, eds. "The Patriot Act Reader: Understanding the Law's Role in the Global War on Terrorism." *Heritage Special Report* SR-01 (September 20, 2004), www.heritage.org/Research/Home landDefense/upload/69895_1.pdf (accessed August 26, 2009).

Schulhofer, Stephen J. *Rethinking the Patriot Act: Ideas for Reform.* New York: Century Foundation, 2005.

Stone, Geoffrey R. *Perilous Times: Free Speech in Wartime from the Sedition Act to the War on Terrorism.* New York: Norton, 2004.

Wong, Kam C. *The Impact of USA PATRIOT Act on American Society: An Evidence-Based Assessment.* Hauppage, NY: Nova Science, 2007.

Index

Page numbers in **boldface** are illustrations, tables, and charts.

About the Author

REBECCA STEFOFF is the author of many nonfiction books for young adults, including *Security v. Privacy* and *The Right to Die* in our Open for Debate series. For the Supreme Court Milestones series, she authored *The Bakke Case: Challenging Affirmative Action*, *Furman v. Georgia: Debating the Death Penalty*, and *U.S. v. Nixon: The Limits of Presidential Privilege*. In addition to books on history, exploration, nature, and science, Stefoff has written on various aspects of social history, including environmental activism and legislation. She also adapted Howard Zinn's best-selling work on American history, *A People's History of the United States*, for young adults. Information about her books for young people is available at www.rebeccastefoff.com.